FROM OBSCURITY TO OBLIVION

LOUIS SANDY MAISEL

FROM OBSCURITY TO OBLIVION

Running in the Congressional Primary

REVISED EDITION

THE UNIVERSITY OF TENNESSEE PRESS : KNOXVILLE

Copyright © 1982 by The University of Tennessee Press / Knoxville
All rights reserved
Manufactured in the United States of America
Revised edition © 1986 by The University of Tennessee Press
Paper: 2nd printing, 1987

Clothbound editions of University of Tennessee Press books are printed on paper designed
for an effective life of at least 300 years, and binding materials are chosen for strength
and durability.

Publication of this book has been aided by a grant from the Lawrence L. Durisch Memorial Fund, administered by the Department of Political Science, The University of Tennessee, Knoxville.

Library of Congress Cataloging in Publication Data
Maisel, Louis Sandy, 1945-
  From obscurity to oblivion.

  Bibliography: p.
  Includes index.
  1. Electioneering—United States.   2. United States.   Congress—Election.
  3. Primaries—United States.   I. Title.
JK1976.M27   324.7'0973   81-21994
ISBN 0-87049-347-7   AACR2
ISBN 0-87049-348-5 (pbk.)

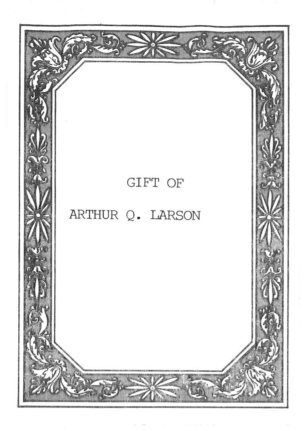

To Dana and Josh —

The gap between generations will never be completely closed. But it must be spanned. For the bridge across the generations is essential to the nation in the present; and more, it is the bridge to our own future — and thus in a central sense, to the very meaning of our own lives.

Robert F. Kennedy

ACKNOWLEDGMENTS

I am one of those who generally read acknowledgments cynically. I have often thought that it would be most honest to say simply, "I wrote this. Others might have added a little, but this is mine." Not true. While this book is mine, while credit or blame should go to me, the research on which it is based would have been impossible without the help of dozens of friends and colleagues. And I was only able to convert that research enterprise into this finished product through the help of many others. In thinking of what those mentioned below have added to this book, I know I will never again read sections such as this one with callous snickers.

First, I want to thank all of those who responded to my questionnaire. Answering took a good deal of time. Many respondents added thoughtful comments that were most helpful. As the respondents have been guaranteed anonymity, I hope they will accept this collective thank you. In addition, those members of Congress and losing candidates whom I personally interviewed, individuals listed in table 1.2, deserve special thanks. These individuals gave freely of their time and opinions; that they permitted me to quote them directly added to the value of those interviews for this book. I am most grateful.

Planning cross-country travel to interview these candidates was a logistical nightmare. Meshing my schedule with the schedules of the candidates and of the airlines would have taxed the most sophisticated computer. Few authors thank their travel agents, but Christol Bluhm of Pieper Travel Service in Buffalo has my sincerest appreciation. So too do my friends and colleagues across the country who helped set up interviews for me and housed and fed me as I toured their areas: Ellen Bayersdorfer, Jane Gellman, Chuck and Vera Jones, Mary Ann and Bill Loweth, Bob and Shannon McArthur, Lynn Olman, Bob Salisbury, Joyce Solo, Catherine Waddell, and Babette Young.

Many students and colleagues, here at Colby and elsewhere, helped me as I collected the data on which this analysis is based and prepared this manuscript. I am especially grateful to Bill Hamilton and Peter Hart, who reviewed the design of my survey; to Jeffra Becknell, Ron Brody, Donna Holt, and Bob Ruzzo, who helped me to collect and analyze primary election returns; to my colleagues in the Government Department at Colby, especially Cal Mackenzie, who served as an invaluable reference source, sounding board, and critical reviewer throughout this project; and to Gary Jacobson and Charles Bullock, whose comments in reviewing the entire manuscript have resulted in what I hope are significant improvements.

I presented a preliminary paper on this topic at the University of Houston-Rice University Conference on Congressional Elections in January 1980. The entire profession owes a debt to David Brady and Joe Cooper for organizing that effort. My debt to them is even greater. Joe Cooper, who has reviewed and criticized this manuscript with his normal thoroughness, has been one of my best friends and severest critics since I was an undergraduate student of his at Harvard, seemingly eons ago. In recent years David Brady has joined Cooper in prodding me to get on with this work. In addition I want to thank all of the participants at the University of Houston-Rice University Conference, especially Sam Patterson, for constructive criticisms that helped me to avoid many errors. A revised version of that paper was published in the *American Politics Quarterly* (Maisel, 1981);[1] I am indebted as well to the anonymous reviewers for that journal, who also saved me from unnecessary mistakes.

Patricia Kick has served as our department secretary during the period of time I have been working on this book. I want to thank her for her efforts on my behalf. Julie Cannon has typed and retyped drafts of this manuscript with amazing speed, skill, and humor. Her efforts, more than any other, have altered the cynical way in which I have viewed others' acknowledgments. That this book appears when it does is due largely to her splendid performance.

---

1. All references are fully cited in the bibliography.

That this book appears at all is in large part due to a series of grants I have received from Colby College. To the members of the Social Science Grants Committee and the Committee on Research, Travel, and Sabbatical for their confidence and to the College for financial support, I am most grateful.

Finally, this book is largely about my own campaign for Congress. Each time I have recalled that experience as I have worked on this book, I have thought about my family and the friends who worked so hard for me on that effort. I have tried to thank them all before. I will undoubtedly do so again. I will never do it adequately. Some of those who helped in my campaign are mentioned in this book. As I write this, I can think of at least another score of people I should have mentioned. I only hope none is slighted and that all realize my enduring gratitude.

This book is dedicated to my daughter, Dana, and my son, Josh. For a year I ran for Congress, I hope they understand why. For another year I worked on this book. Neither of those years was particularly pleasant for my children. They grew a great deal in that time. I think they understand why I am so concerned about our government and the direction it takes. I know they are the ones who will carry that concern forward into the next generation. I am very proud of them. I hope they are proud of what I do as well. And I hope they know that this book is just a small way of telling them how important they are to me.

CONTENTS

TABLES AND CHARTS

CHARTS

FROM
OBSCURITY
TO OBLIVION

1.
INTRODUCTION

On June 13, 1978, I finished fourth in a four-way primary for the Democratic nomination for Congress in Maine's First District. The race was quite close. Fewer than 5,500 votes, fewer than fourteen percentage points, separated the four candidates. Running in a campaign is an intensely personal and emotional experience that permeates every aspect of your life and of the lives of those close to you for months on end. Losing after such a campaign can be devastating, especially if you have second thoughts, the "if only I'd . . ." syndrome.

In the days after my defeat I reexamined my campaign closely. It was a campaign I am proud of. I honestly felt then, and feel now, that there were no important "if only" opportunities, none that would have made a difference: Put simply, I maximized my votes and could not have won. While that conclusion is somewhat reassuring, it has left me with a gnawing question. Why did I not see what was going to happen before it happened? Certainly a campaign as extensive as mine was a valuable learning experience, but that kind of justification is the ultimate rationalization. Given the emotional, physical, and financial toll of the campaign, a toll that I paid and that I asked many others to pay for me, the experience is one I could easily have forgone had I known the conclusion in advance.

I have been troubled by that question, not just as a candidate, but as a political scientist. This book results from probing for answers. Not only did I not foresee what was going to happen, but no one else did either. All around the country sophisticated politicians contest congressional primaries without knowing very much about what they are doing. Political scientists tell students about congressional elections, including primaries, without knowing very much about them. In 1978, 962 candidates ran in contested primaries for a major-party nomination for Congress.[1] Neither politicians nor political scientists know very much about these campaigns, beyond the fact that 795 of them ended in defeat, frequently in a defeat that could and should have been foreseen well in advance.

This book is my effort to explore congressional primaries. It is a very personal book in many ways, the story of my own campaign.[2] I have tried to be analytical in discussing that campaign, but I have also tried to capture feelings and spirit. I believe that those interested in running for office can learn a great deal from a personal account of one who has done it and that students of politics can learn from personal reminiscences and illustrative stories as well as from more rigorous analyses.

At the same time, this book attempts to fill a sizable gap in the professional literature. In recent years scholars have begun to concentrate more attention on elections to Congress. The Survey Research Center at the University of Michigan has taken significant steps toward making more information available so that researchers can examine the various congressional districts. There is a recognition of the fact that we need to know much more about congressional elections if we are to have a full understanding of the representative process. If elections themselves are important, then surely the process through which nominees are chosen is also important. Yet the nominating process is all but unexamined in the professional literature. We know very little about contested primaries generally, even less about those for Congress. We have only the most fragmentary knowledge about those nominations that are decided without contest.[3]

This book, then, goes beyond my own campaign to congressional primaries generally, specifically the primaries of 1978. I gathered infor-

---

1. This and subsequent figures exclude candidates from Louisiana. The "nonpartisan" primary in Louisiana is sufficiently different from the primaries in all other states to make comparisons inappropriate.

2. Christopher Buchanan, who reported on my campaign among many others for *Congressional Quarterly*, has speculated that I entered the congressional primary in order to write this book from personal experience. Let me assure any aspiring authors that the intense effort of a campaign like this one and the high costs, which can be expressed, if not measured, in many different ways, far outweigh any personal benefits that could result from a book like this one.

3. The bibliography at the end of the book lists the most important works that deal with this area even peripherally.

mation on these other primaries in various ways. Shortly after the November election, I mailed a series of questionnaires to those who had run in congressional primaries. The questionnaires sent to incumbents were slightly different from those sent to nonincumbent candidates. The return rate from losers in primaries and from primary winners who lost in November was approximately 34 percent. These respondents matched the total population closely on variables that could be checked; their answers have been used throughout with some confidence. On the other hand, the return rate for incumbents, as expected, was significantly lower. Their answers have been used only for illustrative purposes. The basic questionnaire appears in appendix 1.[4]

In addition, I personally interviewed thirty-nine of these candidates, in nineteen different districts. The interviews ranged from forty-five minutes to three hours in length. All comments were for attribution unless the interviewee specifically requested anonymity on a particular subject. Few did so. I took extensive notes during each interview and reconstructed answers, as closely as I could, immediately after each interview's conclusion. These comments — from winners and losers — allow for amplification on many of the conclusions drawn from the questionnaire responses.

While I felt that this type of data collection was necessary for this project, I must admit that this, too, was something of a personal experience for me. Only 5 of the 179 candidates who challenged incumbents in primaries in 1978 won. In order to oppose incumbents in the general election, the 128 eventual nominees who ran in contested primaries had to beat 219 other candidates. Of these eventual nominees, only 14 won

4. It is perhaps appropriate at the outset to deal with the way the data from my questionnaire have been used throughout this book. Two of those who reviewed earlier versions of this manuscript tempered generally favorable comments with a desire to see more sophisticated statistical analysis using my survey results. In preparing this manuscript I examined the results of the survey in great detail. My conclusion was then and remains now that these data are most useful for descriptive purposes and for the type of analysis that follows. I do not feel they are useful for specific causal analysis. Rather, it is my judgment that going beyond the use I have made of these data tends to trivialize the process; one can see the trees in great detail but loses sight of the forest. Little was added to the knowledge of elections that we already have from those who have studied general elections for Congress (see, for example, Maisel and Cooper, 1981; Jacobson, 1980; Jones, 1967; 1966). The importance of the individual political environments for primaries is more apparent from the examination of the contexts of individual campaigns than from cumulative data. In deciding how to use these data, I was particularly influenced by the comments of Heinz Eulau. In responding to an earlier paper I wrote using these data, Eulau noted that while I broke no new methodological grounds, it was apparent that I understood politics more than most analysts. I hope he meant that as a positive comment; I took it as such and am grateful for it. It is clear to me that the use I have made of my survey data is helpful in explaining politics even if it is a somewhat unusual approach for a political scientist.

Table 1.1   **Congressional Candidates in 1978**

	Democrats	*Republicans*
Incumbent winner unopposed in both primary and general	27	16
Incumbent winner opposed in primary not in general	15	0
Opponents of these incumbents	22	0
Incumbent winner unopposed in primary, opposed in general	119	85
Nominated to oppose these without contested primary	48	86
Nominated to oppose these with contested primary	37	33
Lost contested primary in these districts	60	49
Incumbent winner opposed in both primary and general election	70	19
Lost primary to incumbent in these races	120	21
Nominated to oppose these without contested primary	7	38
Nominated to oppose these with contested primary	12	32
Lost primary to oppose incumbent in these districts	25	51
New member beat incumbent in general after winning primary	4	10
Lost primary to eventual winner	8	26
Incumbent who lost was nominated without primary opposition	7	3
Incumbent who lost had primary	3	1
Lost to incumbent who eventually lost	4	1
New member nominated without primary beat incumbent in general	1	4

when facing the incumbent in November. (Table 1.1 summarizes the electoral paths followed by congressional candidates in 1978.) That creates an incredibly bleak prospect for those seeking to enter Congress through the dual process of winning a contested primary and a general election. I knew the picture was bleak before I decided to run, but I am

Table 1.1 (continued)

	Democrats	Republicans
Incumbent who lost had no primary	2	1
Incumbent who lost had contested primary	2	0
Lost to incumbent who eventually lost	6	0
Open seat; new member had primary	33	16
Incumbent lost in primary to eventual new member	4	0
Incumbent lost in primary though new member in other party	1	0
Losers to new members in primary	109	40
Losers to new members in general; nominated without primary	1	19
Losers to new members in general; nominated with primary	15	14
Losers to candidate who lost to new member in general	54	33
Open seat; new members had no primary	3	5
Losers nominated without primary	1	3
Losers nominated with primary	4	0
Losers to those nominated in primary above	8	0
Incumbent winners in Louisiana's "nonpartisan" primary	4	2
Losers to these	7	2*
Incumbent winner in Louisiana with no opposition	0	1
Open seat winner in Louisiana's "nonpartisan" primary	1	0
Lost runoff to above	0	1
Losers in primary	7	0

*An additional two losers listed no party.

still not certain that I ever squarely faced how truly dark it was.

Many people think about running for Congress. If one thinks about it loudly enough, the press will even report those thoughts. That in itself is an ego-trip for many would-be candidates. But a tremendous psychological barrier separates thinking about running from running. I wanted to meet the men and women who crossed that barrier, to probe their

Table 1.2 **Candidates in Districts in which Interviews Were Conducted**

State	District	Candidates	Party	Codes*
California	14	Norma Lowry	D	
		John J. McFall	D	2,4
		Carl Burton	R	
		Irenemaree Castillo	R	
		Charles M. Gibson	R	
		L. Allen Kreiss, Jr.	R	
		James W. Pinkerton, Jr.	R	
		Norman D. Shumway	R	1,3
		Fred S. Van Dyke	R	
Illinois	10	Abner J. Mikva	D	2,5
		Daniel B. Hales	R	
		Richard Janecek	R	1
		Mark H. "Markus" Johnson	R	
		Peter C. Pierce	R	
		John E. Porter	R	1,4
		Eugene R. Salamon	R	1
		David Thompson	R	
Indiana	6	David W. Evans	D	2,5
		Chester Coomer	R	
		David G. Crane	R	4
		A. T. (Skip) Lange	R	1
		Philip J. Thorpe	R	
Indiana	7	Raymond R. Cronin	D	
		James M. Mason	D	
		Dallas Meneely	D	
		Billy R. Pearman	D	
		John W. Tipton	D	
		Charlotte Zietlow	D	1,4
		Ernest R. Boykin	R	
		John T. Myers	R	2,3
Kentucky	4	John F. Hudak	D	
		Jim Lawrence	D	1
		George C. Martin	D	4
		Gene Snyder	R	2,5

motivations, to assess their reactions to campaigning, to compare their experiences with mine. (Table 1.2 lists all of the candidates in the districts in which I conducted personal interviews.)

One of the reasons that congressional elections and primaries have been so understudied is that congressional districts are tremendously varied

Table 1.2 (continued)

State	District	Candidates	Party	Codes*
Maine	1	Louis Sandy Maisel	D	
		Guy A. Marcotte	D	1
		John Quinn	D	1,4
		Richard A. Spencer	D	1
		David F. Emery	R	2,5
Mississippi	4	James D. Disharoon	D	
		Melvin R. Jennings	D	
		Ken Johnson	D	
		Mike Marks	D	
		Bob Mitchell	D	
		John Hampton Stennis	D	4
		D. A. "Doug" Tuttle	D	
		Craig Gibson	R	
		Jon C. Hinson	R	1,3
		Gray Jackson	R	
Missouri	1	William (Bill) Clay	D	1,2,3
		Helen L. Gerleman	D	
		Benjamin L. Goins	D	
		Elsa Debra Hill	D	
		Felix J. Panlasigui	D	
		Barry Shelton	D	
		Takuri Tei	D	
		Richard H. Riley	R	
		Bill White	R	1,4
Ohio	2	Thomas A. Luken	D	2,5
		Stanley J. Aronoff	R	
		Thearon O. "Tom" Atkins	R	1,4
Ohio	19	Charles J. Carney	D	2,4
		Vincent E. Gilmartin	D	1
		George E. Tablack	D	1
		Gary J. Thompson	D	
		John Scott Hay	R	
		Joseph J. Rohan	R	1
		Gary L. Van Brocklin	R	1
		Lyle Williams	R	1,3

in terms of geography, demographics, political complexion, and like factors; thus they do not lend themselves easily to generalization. A book about one campaign could be illustrative, but it could not be very useful for obtaining a more pervasive knowledge of the process under study. By

Table 1.2 (continued)

State	District	Candidates	Party	Codes*
Oklahoma	2	Ted Risenhoover	D	2
		Mike Synar	D	1,3
		Gary Richardson	R	
Pennsylvania	1	Robert G. Allman	D	1
		Stanley E. Branche	D	1
		George G. Britt	D	1
		Julius E. Curry	D	
		Andrew DiAntonia	D	
		Robert J. Mulligan	D	
		Michael Myers	D	2,3
		Samuel N. Fanelli	R	
Pennsylvania	4	Mark B. Cohen	D	1
		Paul D. Corbett	D	
		Joshua Eilberg	D	2,4
		Aloysius E. Stuhl	D	
		Charles F. Dougherty	R	5
Pennsylvania	21	Don Bailey	D	3
		John A. Cicco, Jr.	D	1
		Edward F. Cooke	D	
		June DePietro	D	1
		Richard C. Grove	D	
		Richard A. Halapin	D	
		James R. Kelley	D	
		James J. Manderino	D	
		Joseph A. Petrarca	D	
		Bernard F. Scherer	D	
		Donald C. Thomson	D	
		Richard F. Miaskiewicz	R	
		Robert H. Miller	R	1,4
		David L. Robinson	R	1
		George E. Saxon	R	
Tennessee	5	Bill Boner	D	3
		Porter Freeman	D	1
		Charles Galbreath	D	1
		Jeannine Honicker	D	1
		Red McEwen	D	
		Elliot Ozment	D	1
		Bill Goodwin	R	4
		Roy Allan Stranaham	R	

Table 1.2 (continued)

State	District	Candidates	Party	Codes*
Texas	8	Joe Archer	D	
		Bob Eckhardt	D	2,3
Texas	18	Anthony Hall	D	1
		Mickey Leland	D	3
		Jack Linville,Jr.	D	
		Judson Robinson, Jr.	D	
		Harrel Tillman	D	
		Al Vera	D	1
		Nat West	D	
Texas	22	Bob Gammage	D	1,2,4
		Gerald Liedtke	D	
		Mike Richards	D	
		George Steward	D	
		Ron Paul	R	5
Texas	24	Martin Frost	D	1,3
		Dale Milford	D	2
		Leo Berman	R	4
		Ben F. Bruce	R	

*1 = interviewed
2 = incumbent
3 = won primary and general election

4 = won primary, lost general election
5 = won general, nominated without a primary

gathering data on a large number of campaigns across the country and by supplementing my own personal recollections with those of other candidates, I feel that the contribution of this book has been enhanced.

If the genesis of this book was the question, ''Why didn't my fellow political scientists prepare me more fully for the campaign I was to run?'' then the logical corollary question was,''Why did I decide to run in the first place?'' I am not at all certain that I will ever really know the answer to that, but that question is where this book starts. Political scientists have only begun to explore the question of why someone seeks office (Huckshorn and Spencer, 1971; Fishel, 1973; Kazee, 1980). In chapter 2, I explore my own motivation in running for Congress and compare it with the reasons others have given for contesting primaries. In addition to examining motivations, I also attempt to explain how the decision to run is made and when it is made. In that discussion two of the themes repeated throughout this book are raised.

First, two of the most overworked phrases in the cliché-ridden literature on American politics should be permanently retired. This nation is in love with sports, but inaccurate analogies should not be continued simply because they conjure up clear pictures in the popular mind. There is no such thing as a "political season" Arthur Hadley (1976) and Jules Witcover (1977) both accurately point out that the presidential campaign of 1976 actually began at least four years earlier. The same can be said for congressional campaigns — the quest for office begins at least two years and sometimes many more years than that — before the actual election. Candidates and would-be candidates plot and plan and posture. Politicians are aware of much of this activity. Journalists dub the "political season" as that period during which this activity becomes public. To a large extent that season is defined by when journalists decide to devote their efforts to covering it. It is an artificial construct of the reporting of politics and arbitrarily separates one period in a campaign from another to which it is logically connected. Visible campaigns last but a few months — and many feel that that is too long — but they represent only a small fraction of the total political activity that leads to a nomination and an election.

Similarly, the racing analogy should be buried forever. Witcover (1977: x) admits that the horse race analogy is overworked but tries to revive it by showing that a candidate for the presidency must be like a jockey in the early going of a race, constantly looking for openings, changing strategy to meet changing situations, and the like. He does an even greater disservice by naming his book *Marathon*. In a horse race, in a marathon, in a 200-meter dash, in almost any race one can name, the contestants start at the same place and end at the same place. They travel the same course. They must overcome the same obstacles. None of these parallels holds for political contests.

Candidates start campaigning at different times. They start with different resources. They start from different places in terms of how close they are to eventual success. They travel different courses. They have different obstacles to overcome. The inelegance of the analogy can be extended much further, and others have criticized it as well. Yet it persists. Throughout this book, from the examination of the decision to run on, one sees over and over again how it fails and how deserving of retirement it is.

The second theme introduced in chapter 2 and reiterated through the book relates to the number of decisions that are made in political campaigns, particularly in primary campaigns, based on totally inadequate information. Fenno (1978: 17) points out that incumbents seeking reelection often make campaign decisions in ignorance. I am certain this is even more true of challengers. To point to the most basic type of information gap, when I first decided to enter the First District primary, only one other candidate, State Representative Richard Spencer, was certain to contest the nomination. In 1976, seven Democrats had entered the primary to oppose then-freshman Republican Representative David Emery. I knew that none of those seven planned a repeat campaign in 1978. I was quite certain that Peter Kyros, who had held this seat from 1967 until he was upset by Emery in the 1974 election, was unlikely to return to Maine from Washington to attempt a political comeback. I knew that none of the Democrats who had opposed Kyros in previous primaries was interested in the 1978 nomination. I knew absolutely nothing about the intentions of either John Quinn or Guy Marcotte, the two men who later became candidates and finished first and second in the primary. How could information be more inadequate? I entered the primary without knowing the most basic piece of information — who my opponents would be. Dick Spencer had to make his decision with even less information than I had, for he did not know I was running. Neither of us could have waited much longer than we did, certainly not until the time when the others decided to seek the nomination, because of where we started and the obstacles we had to overcome.

In any campaign a candidate has a certain amount of resources, and he or she must decide how to allocate those resources. Some can be expended to gain more information on which to base decisions. In primary campaigns, resources tend to be more limited than in general elections. In congressional campaigns, they tend to be more limited than in campaigns for statewide or national offices. Only rarely can congressional candidates afford to expend their limited resources to commission a professional poll of their district. Consequently, most make decisions concerning how the voters feel with only intuitive information. In some cases information gaps can be filled through reallocation of campaign resources. But in many cases the information that one would like in order to make a rational decision simply does not exist. One lasting impression from my campaign, despite the fact that I have had a good deal of political experience and tried to run my campaign in a professional manner, was the frequency of the need to make "seat of the pants" decisions.

After the discussion of the decision to run in chapter 2, various other aspects of the campaign itself are presented. In each case my own experience is examined in some depth and then compared with the experiences of others around the country. This analysis points to the range of possible experiences, the differences among congressional districts, and how these differences lead to differing campaign practices.

Chapter 3 is an examination of campaign organization — or lack thereof. One of the highlights of my campaign was reading a newspaper account of "the army of Maisel volunteers throughout the district." I asked my campaign manager how she felt to command such a potent force. She replied that the power of "blue smoke and mirrors" never ceased to amaze her. This chapter discusses what type and size of an organization one needs and what variables determine that. It also highlights the difference between the appearance and the reality of organization.

Financial debt is a subject with which most contestants in congressional primaries — especially losers — are familiar. Chapter 4 looks at the process through which I built my debt. Nowhere is the inadequacy of information more apparent than in reaching decisions on funding a campaign. Budgetary decisions are very important, and no one takes them lightly. In retrospect, however, I shudder when I think of how I reached decisions about how much I would spend and how it would be allocated, about how much money I could raise and where I would raise it, about how complicated financial reporting requirements were and how much time my treasurer would have to spend in assuring that we complied with Federal Election Commission regulations. My faith in my own ability to make judgments is only slightly restored by the knowledge that others underestimated these problems in much the same way I did.

Chapter 5 deals with the appeals made during the campaign, with campaign strategy. How does one decide what themes one should emphasize, what message one wants to get across, what image one wants to portray? These are important decisions for a campaign. They are important decisions for candidates as individuals — and as potential officeholders. In examining these questions, any candidate must become introspective. The candidate must reflect on his or her own principles, on what he or she wants to do in office, on how much he or she is willing to compromise in order to win an election. One has to deal with questions concerning what comprises one's natural constituency, whether that is a winning constituency or not, and, if not, what one must do to expand it.

Chapter 6 discusses the tactics used during a campaign. How can a candidate's message be transmitted? What do you do with paid media? How do you handle the press? What does your campaign literature look like? These are all important questions. We spent a good deal of time on them in my campaign. Any candidate should, because most candidates lose, and for the losers these kinds of memories are what remain after the debt is paid. This chapter also answers my ex-mother-in-law, who kept asking, ''What did you do this week?'' Few people know what candidates do with their time. Few candidates know before they actually campaign. We read about the eighteen-to-twenty hour days that candidates spend. We rarely know what goes on in those days. Few observers realize that many others working on a campaign are spending as much time. Chapter 6 looks at the activities of candidates and of campaign workers. Where does the time go? What is the effect of spending that much time?

Nothing in my personal experience has even approximated the sustained physical and emotional crescendo of the last week of my primary campaign. Nothing has ever provided such a contrast as the feeling of cleaning out an office after losing. Chapter 7 deals with the intensity of the last week of a campaign, with how one loses a sense of reality both as to the actual situation and as to the importance of what is happening, with how one picks up the pieces after it is over. I have always been amazed at the lack of in-depth postelection analysis. Winners seem to feel that it should be obvious to everyone that they won because they were the best candidate. Losers never have the energy — or the resources — and rarely have the motivation — or the heart — to examine why they were rejected. In this chapter I have given one explanation of why my election turned out as it did. In so doing, I was once again made acutely aware of how intensely personal a campaign is; for I am not at all certain that I demanded of myself the analytical rigor in this situation that I would have demanded in another.

The final chapter then turns to some of the important public-policy questions raised by the way in which we nominate candidates for Congress. Two concerns are paramount. First, what is the significance of the fact that so many nominations are uncontested, that many incumbents are challenged neither in primaries nor in the general election? Second, what of the primaries that are held? What effect do they have on the general elections, on our representative system? How would the primaries be changed or how would this effect be altered if we went to a system of publicly financing congressional primaries?

Some of my colleagues have warned me that it is not possible to write a book that is at the same time a personal account of one's own experience in a campaign and an analytical account of the process of which that campaign was a part. I feel that there is a need for both kinds of books and that the format I have chosen is appropriate. The accuracy of my perception is reflected in the extent to which readers of this book come away with a feeling of what a campaign means to the candidate involved and of the range of experiences found in congressional primaries throughout the country.

2.
THE DECISION
TO RUN

Anyone who has seen Jimmy Stewart in *Mr. Smith Goes to Washington* knows why I ran for Congress. Jefferson Smith arrives by train at Union Station. He sees the Capitol dome and is drawn toward it. He is oblivious to all around him, lost in the history and symbolism of Washington. That scene may well be the corniest of all the trite statements moviemakers have made about blind patriotism. But in a real sense, the aura of Washington, the sense of history, the call of patriotism draws many into the political arena.

I remember well when I first decided to run for Congress. I was a college intern in the office of Richard D. McCarthy (D., N.Y., 1965-71). The congressman gave me a tour of the Capitol, took me onto the floor, introduced me to the speaker, and entertained me in the members' dining room. I knew right then that I wanted to sit in the House on my own someday. That feeling was reinforced every time I flew into Washington, especially when I landed at night, descending over the Potomac with the Washington Monument, the Lincoln and Jefferson memorials, and the Capitol all spotlighted below. I twice lived in Washington for short periods, working on congressional staffs. Those experiences also rekindled my desire to run on my own. Service on a congressional staff only proves more conclusively that members alone are at the center of the real action. Experiences such as mine do not appear to be uncommon. One of those I interviewed commented: "My entry into politics was from a feeling of conscience. I had the time, the money, and maybe some ability. I had time and I had money. And I always felt that we all owe something to our country. So I decided I'd run for Congress."[1]

Four of the members of the Ninety-sixth Congress first came to Washington as congressional pages. Their decisions to run were made at very early ages. Jon Hinson (R., Miss., 1979-81) is one of those: "I came up here in 1959 as a page. That decided it was for me. I knew right then that I wanted to run for Congress eventually."

The key, however, is the step from running for Congress "eventually" to running in a particular election. In most cases the decision seems to be partly analytical and partly emotional. It is difficult to draw the line between the two.

David Emery, who represents the First Congressional District in Maine, is a young, if somewhat uninspiring, Republican. Emery won the seat in 1974, upsetting Peter Kyros (D., Me.,1967-75). In the 1974 election Emery, then twenty-six years old, was one of only four Republicans to beat incumbent Democrats. Kyros had systematically alienated large portions of his constituents through dogged defense of our policy in Vietnam and reputedly questionable personal behavior. Three times he had withstood bitter primary challenges, the last by a woman who had served on his staff and who used her detailed knowledge of his congressional service against him. Despite Kyros's difficulties, most observers felt he was safe. Emery won the Republican nomination without opposition. Few gave him any chance at all, feeling that the Republicans had put him up as a sacrificial lamb. Emery's campaign was badly under financed, so he reverted to a person-to-person approach, starting early and working very hard. Most of the attention in 1974 was focused on the campaign for governor, in which Independent James Longley defeated Democrat George Mitchell (now Maine's junior senator) and Republican James Erwin. Longley's surprise victory was coupled with Emery's upset of Kyros by a margin of only 679 votes out of almost 200,000 cast.

Kyros demanded a recount and challenged Emery's right to be seated in the House. Emery's victory was upheld at every level. Kyros acquired a new negative image, that of a poor loser. As for Emery, no sooner was he seated than campaigns started against him. Democrats in Maine viewed the seat as highly winnable. In all, seven Democrats entered the

---

1. This and other quotations throughout this book are taken from the interviews I conducted with congressional candidates. While all interviews were "on the record" for attribution, I have only identified the respondents for those quotes for which such attribution added to the point under discussion.

1976 primary to oppose Emery, who again faced no primary competition. (Kyros failed to qualify for the ballot after deciding late that he would run; irregularities were found in those petitions he did file.) The Democratic primary was highly divisive. The eventual winner, Rick Barton, who had been an aide to Senator William Hathaway, never successfully united the party. Emery defeated him handily, winning by over 37,000 votes, 57 to 43 percent.

While Emery's legislative record in the House was not overly impressive, his office was doing an effective job of constituent service. In viewing my decision to run for Congress "eventually," I looked at 1978 as maybe the last chance at this seat in the foreseeable future.

Emery still seemed "vulnerable," but it was questionable how long that vulnerability would last. I was all too familiar with the political science literature on the ability of members of Congress to use their service in the House to create a safe seat from one that had been marginal (Mayhew, 1974a; Ferejohn, 1977; see also the articles generated by the 1978 Survey Research Center study, for example, Maisel and Cooper, 1981). Thus, one part of my analytical equation, the part dealing with the potential for a Democrat to take the seat, said 1978 was a "now-or-never" year.

Before deciding to run, I had to know not only whether any Democrat could take the seat but also whether I was the Democrat who could do so. Such personal evaluations are never easy. In my case I knew that I was not a native, that I was a college professor, and that I was Jewish in a district with few Jews. I knew full well that none of these factors would help; I also knew that I had a political base in Maine, that I had no plans to move to build another political base, and that none of the negative factors was going to change. Therefore, in terms of evaluating my personal prospects in the district, I certainly could not be positive, but nothing was likely to change to make my prospects more positive at a later date.

Next I viewed the primary field. A repeat of the 1976 intraparty battle would lead inevitably to another Emery victory. I talked to each of the 1976 contenders; none was going to try again. Peter Kyros had not returned to Maine in nearly four years; he did not seem to be a factor. The only active candidate was State Representative Richard Spencer, an appealing liberal from the Portland area. Clearly Spencer was a strong candidate, but not invincible. His major advantages were holding public office — but was that really an advantage in the post-Watergate age? — and wealth — and that was an advantage. I talked with him. He seemed a lot like me; he had gone to Harvard, had moved to Maine about the time I had, and could not hide his political ambition. He knew politics and had good contacts. His evaluation of the district was similar to mine, and he too knew that a bitter primary would cripple the winner. We made a pact that if we both entered, we would follow the Republicans' Eleventh Commandment — not to speak ill of each other. Final assessment: if 1978 was my best shot, Dick Spencer was not going to scare me out.

I made all of these assessments during the spring of 1977 when I was working in Washington on the staff of the House of Representatives Commission on Administrative Review (the Obey Commission) and commuting to Maine on weekends. More than once when I boarded a Delta Airlines plane at National Airport, I saw Dave Emery getting on the same plane. We nodded politely, and I kept thinking, "You wouldn't be so friendly if you knew what was in my mind." Then I began to worry that perhaps he could not care less. After all, who was Sandy Maisel? Did others in the district really feel I had a chance? Who can you turn to?

I spent three weekends in the early summer trying to answer those questions, seeking advice from politicians whose judgment I trusted. Always I asked the same question: does a liberal, Jewish, college professor from Buffalo have any business thinking about running for Congress from Maine's First District?

The answers I received varied widely. George Mitchell felt my religion would not be a detriment. He said that Jews were such a minority in Maine that no one feared them. By implication he was also saying that his own Lebanese background, in a state with a large Lebanese minority, had hurt his chances to win the governorship in 1974. I knew that was so in Waterville, but I was less certain of his advice to me.

Jim Mitchell, no relation to George, had run second to Rick Barton in 1976. He still yearned to be a congressman, but said he would not run unless he found a sugar daddy. He had only begun to pay off a large debt. Mitchell, whose wife served in the legislature with Spencer and was active in his campaign, professed that he would be neutral in this race. His conclusion was that Spencer would be a formidable opponent because of his money, and further that neither of us could touch Emery. I discounted that advice because it was not what I wanted to hear.

Next I went to Gordon Weil. Weil, who was executive assistant to George McGovern during the 1972 presidential campaign, is generally thought to be the wisest politician in the state. He scoffs at such accolades. "I told my son that the parade was starting again. Last time all seven came to see me. I gave them all advice. None followed it. But I'm not so sure I was wise anyhow." Weil said he would help me, though he would not run my campaign. He also said that my chances were as good as anyone's and that, if I was going to run, I should get at it. He agreed with my view that a highly visible door-to-door campaign with young volunteers might do the trick.

And my discussions went on and on. I talked at length with Kevin and Nancy Hill, wonderful friends, savvy politicians, wise counselors.

They said they would cochair my campaign committee and help in Waterville. They said if I was going to run, they would be part of the effort. But they questioned why I was going to do it. Why did I want to inflict that on myself?

I talked with students at Colby and on other campuses to see if I could mount the volunteer effort I felt I needed. I talked with prominent Jewish leaders to see if they would help me raise money. I touched all the necessary bases — party officials, prominent citizens, unions, fundraisers, everyone I could think of. I debated the issue with my family, having others play the devil's advocate. During these debates I realized that the issue had already been settled.

As a practical politician and a knowledgeable student of politics, I knew the analytical questions I had to ask. So I asked them, but I did not really care what the answers were. My experience in Washington, my gut instinct that 1978 was my one best chance to grab the golden ring, and the incredible "high" I felt each time anyone said something supportive all told me I was going to run. The "decisionmaking" process I was going through was something of a sham. I was looking for some hard evidence to tell me that the decision I had already made in my heart made sense. The emotional decision to run was made well before the intellectual one. That personal commitment in fact was probably too strong to be overcome by rational analysis. So I still cannot answer — even with three years of hindsight and reflection — when I decided to run for Congress in 1978. It is somewhat humbling to realize that a career of professional training probably played little part in reaching that decision.

When I reviewed my campaign shortly after its conclusion, I was amazed by how little I knew when I decided to run. I did not know who my opponents would be; I did not know how I was perceived throughout the district, by the political leaders or by those at the grass roots; I did not know how much money I could raise, nor what others could spend against me; I did not know how my most strongly felt views would be received by the electorate; I did not know in a precise way what Emery's weaknesses were. The list could be expanded. Some of this information became clearer to me in the fall of 1977, when I commissioned a poll of the district. That was before I formally announced my candidacy, but well after the time when I knew I was in to stay.

The retrospective view of my own lack of information led me to wonder whether others also made so major a decision with just as little knowledge. Approximately 30 percent of those running in contested primaries in 1978 made their firm decision to run right after the 1976 election. The next biggest group of candidates made their decisions in the late fall of 1977, less than a year before their primaries. When that

Table 2.1 The Relationship Between the Time of Firm Decision to Run and Success in Congressional Primaries

TIME OF FIRM DECISION*	Total	Open Seat		To Challenge Incumbent in Other Party		Against Incumbent in Own Party	
		Won	Lost	Won	Lost	Won	Lost
Late 1976	31.1%	50.0%	16.7%	14.3%	43.8%	0	37.5%
Fall 1977	68.9%	50.0%	83.3%	85.7%	56.3%***	0	62.5%
N =	45	2	12	7	16	0	8

(N = 45)

*See question I.2 on the questionnaire in appendix I for the exact wording of the question and answers.

**Where it has been deemed relevant, primary candidates have been divided according to whether they were running for an open seat (a seat in which the incumbent was not seeking reelection in 1978), in a primary to gain their party's nomination to oppose an incumbent of the other party, or in a primary against an incumbent in their own party. The "Total" column cumulates the six subcategories.

***Percentages do not total 100 because of rounding.

decision was made seemed to have little effect on whether or not the candidates won their primaries.

Those who decided earliest tended to be the candidates previously active in congressional races. They were knowledgeable about the district and made their decisions based on factors relating to the district, not to their own candidacy. Congressman Hinson, as an example,decided to run as soon as he suspected the seat in Mississippi's Fourth District might be vacant. When Thad Cochran (R., Miss., 1973-79) first decided he might run for the Senate, he "made a calculated decision and went home to Mississippi to prepare to run. . . . At the point when I knew Cochran would run and the seat would be vacant, I decided that I'd try to get support and wouldn't be scared out by any individual."

Two unsuccessful candidates, the first from Illinois and the second from Pennsylvania, decided early for similar reasons.

When Sam lost in 1976, well you can't really lose twice in a row within two years and be a serious contender for the same office. At that time I figured the nomination was available and I'd go for it.

I would have run no matter what Dent did. I ran against Johnny two years ago. I'd run a strong race two years prior and I felt, with his added health problems, he was vulnerable.

These candidates did not know about all their 1978 opponents when they made the firm commitment to run. In fact, the second losing candidate quoted above concluded, "I might have done better against an ailing incumbent than a fresh face."

Table 2.2 **Means of Assessing Primary Chances**

ASSESSMENT OF PRIMARY CHANCES*	Total	TYPE OF CANDIDATE**					
		Open Seat		To Challenge Incumbent in Other Party		Against Incumbent in Own Party	
		Won	Lost	Won	Lost	Won	Lost
Political Intuition	45.3%	50.0%	39.4%	43.2%	41.0%	0	60.4%
Discussion with Political Leaders	19.1%	40.0%	16.9%	34.1%	19.2%	0	4.2%
Political Intuition and Discussion with Political Leaders	19.5%***	10.0%	22.5%***	15.9%	26.9%***	0	8.3%
Media Assessment	2.0%	0	3.0%	0	3.8%	0	0
Poll	8.3%	0	15.5%	2.3%	3.8%	0	12.5%
Other	6.0%	0	2.8%	4.5%	5.1%	0	14.6%
N =	251	10	71	44	78	0	48

(N = 251)
*See question I.8 on the questionnaire in appendix I for the exact wording of the question and answers.
**See note with table 2.1.
***Percentages do not total 100 because of rounding.

Those who decided later that they were going to run had more chance to read the lay of the land, but they too were faced with some uncertainty. Over 40 percent of those polled in 1978 were not certain of who their major opponents would eventually be when they decided to run. Often this knowledge would have changed the decision.

I announced in March. That's when I decided. I guess I honestly felt Tablack would withdraw. His term in Columbus was up. He had to give up a lot to run for Congress. I thought in the end he'd figure he was giving up too much.

I probably wouldn't have run if he'd said he was. I wouldn't have felt I had the name recognition.

If I had known Miller was going to get in initially, I think it would have kept me out. I went to him because he was the most likely candidate. He said he didn't know but he didn't think he was going to do it. Then the time came; I got in. He was still professing he wasn't sure. Finally he decided, and the rest is history.

It seemed logical to ask why people did not have this kind of information when they entered a major race. To some extent it is because they did not seek it. Table 2.2 reveals that nearly half of those polled, 45.2 percent, relied on their own political intuition when assessing their chances of winning the primary. Another fifth relied on a combination of their political intuition and the views of political leaders. If my personal experience was typical, the political intuition aspect of the equation weighed much more heavily. Another fifth relied heavily on political leaders; fewer than 10 percent conducted polls before assessing their chances. Obviously, if the decision was made in advance based on factors other than a realistic assessment of chance of winning, then seeking further information had little payoff.

However, other factors also intervened. As mentioned earlier, all candidates do not start at the same place. Some, if they were to have any chance, had to start early even though they did not have all of the information they desired. Others, because of previous exposure, party backing, personal wealth, or other reasons, could wait much longer. The situation of Skip Lange, who ran against Dr. David Crane, is typical. Crane had run before, was enormously wealthy, and was known as part of a potent Midwest Republican family. Lange had no such advantages: "I talked to Crane in January of 1977. At that time I wasn't committed and neither was he. I decided to go to the primary for sure in February of 1977, when those party dinners started. I had to get known by the regulars. I felt he might go, but he hadn't said so. He didn't announce until midsummer, to avoid some filing requirements I think."

On the other hand, some potential candidates did a tremendous amount of research before they entered their races. Charlotte Zietlow, who ran in Indiana's Seventh District, explained the process she followed: "I went to Washington and I talked to the whole Indiana delegation, especially to Floyd Fithian and Phil Sharpe because their districts are similar to this one. Eventually we even put out a booklet called 'Why Charlotte Can Win' in which we outlined our strategy. We used it for fundraising later on."

Others made the decision to run, filed their candidacy, but never fully committed themselves personally. The following examples, the first taken from the Nineteenth District in Ohio and the second from the First District in Pennsylvania, illustrate a different level of commitment to running than that discussed earlier:

> I got out of the race before I raised or spent a cent. I thought Gilmartin or Tablack would beat Carney. There was no way I wanted to run against either of them. This is a heavily Democratic seat, and they would have been unbeatable.

> I filed in 1978 again. I was hoping not too many would get in, but they did. I didn't campaign at all this time. When I saw all of those filing I knew I couldn't win, so I didn't work at all.

Throughout this discussion the assumption that one runs for Congress with the thought of winning has been implicit. I think I made that assumption initially because winning certainly was my motivation. However, it is an assumption that is testable and proves to be false.

Nearly a quarter of those responding to my questionnaire said that at the time they filed, they felt that their chances of winning their primaries were remote at best. Another quarter felt that they had only a fair chance of winning the primary. In addition, about 40 percent felt they had a fair chance at best of winning in November, even if they won the primary.

Politicians tend to have an incredible ability to delude themselves about their own chances. If I could honestly think that a young, liberal, Jewish college professor from Buffalo could win a primary and then beat a popular incumbent in Downeast Maine, any level of delusion is possible. Many of the candidates I interviewed convinced themselves that their toughest opponent would not run. They entered the race and never reexamined their assumptions or the consequences if those assumptions proved to be wrong. Others had a more realistic outlook.

In Pennsylvania the statehouse is not a very good stepping stone. We don't get much media coverage. We don't have staff resources, and we're not perceived as very powerful. I thought I had a 40 to 50 percent chance of winning, based mainly on resentment of Eilberg.

I thought I had an outside chance to win. I knew Leland was being endorsed by everyone and realized what that meant. But I'm not a party man. I looked at the makeup of the district and thought that just maybe there were enough people not associated with political interests to pull it off.

Many of the 962 primary candidates entered their races feeling that winning was beyond their grasp or only a remote possibility. Why did they do it? Why did they do it in 1978? Table 2.3 lists responses to the question, "Many people desire to serve in Congress, but far fewer take the major step of actually running. Assuming your desire to serve, why did you decide to run in 1978?"

Two themes seem to emerge. Candidates ran because it was something they knew they were going to do sometime and, for whatever reasons, 1978 appeared to be the right time. Or, candidates ran because of their feelings on certain issues, to air their views, to present an alternative. Jeannine Honicker in Nashville ran because she was committed to a cause: "It all started with my involvement in the anti-nuclear-power movement. . . . I didn't think I'd fare as well as I did. People say I came out good on the issues on television. . . . Mine was not a successful campaign in terms of winning votes, but it is the cheapest way in the world to get your issue heard.

Table 2.3 Reasons for Running for Congress

WHY RUN?*	Total	Open Seat		To Challenge Incumbent in Other Party		Against Incumbent in Own Party	
		Won	Lost	Won	Lost	Won	Lost
Certain Victory	4.0%	10.0%	6.9%	2.3%	2.6%	0	2.1%
Best Chance to Win	21.0%	40.0%	25.0%	22.7%	19.5%	0	12.5%
Obligation to Provide Alternative	31.1%	0	20.8%	45.5%	29.9%	0	43.8%
Had to do it	13.9%	20.0%	25.0%	4.5%	9.1%	0	10.4%
Good Professionally	2.4%	10.0%	2.8%	4.5%	1.3%	0	0
Help Build Base	9.1%	0	4.2%	13.6%	13.0%	0	8.3%
Need to Air Views	12.3%	10.0%	11.1%	4.5%	15.6%	0	16.7%
Other	6.0%***	10.0%	4.2%	0	9.1%***	0	6.3%***
N =	252	10	72	44	77	0	48

(N = 252)
*See question I.10 on the questionnaire in appendix I for the exact wording of the question and answers.
**See note with table 2.1.
***Percentages do not total 100 because of rounding.

Houston Republicans (and oil interests) know that Bob Eckhardt is popular, but they also feel a viable alternative can beat him:

It's important that there be a Republican alternative, and I think a Republican can win. Lance Tarrance's surveys showed for the first time this district is conservative. A Republican can win it. When George Bush was running against Lloyd Bentsen, he almost carried it. . . . Archer [Eckhardt's primary opponent in 1978] would be a liberal in the House after his first term. He tried to paint himself conservative, but he's liberal. . . . I'm not even sure I'd like it in Congress, but I kept thinking I'd be better than Eckhardt.

Thus, for a variety of reasons, 962 individuals decided to enter primary elections to run for Congress in 1978. Another 474 individuals received major-party nominations without contested primaries. The field was crowded. There was no shortage of job applicants in many districts. However, it is important to note that the phenomenon of competition was not spread uniformly throughout the country.

Recent literature on congressional elections (see, as examples, Abramowitz, 1981; Hinckley, 1981; Mann and Wolfinger, 1981; Parker, 1980; 1981; Payne, 1980) has emphasized that incumbents have a

Table 2.4 **Incumbents' Success in Congressional Elections***

Year	Percent of Nominated Incumbents Reelected in General Election	Number Defeated in Primary	Number Defeated in General Election
1960	93.50	6	26
1962	94.34	12	22
1964	88.43	5	45
1966	90.05	11	40
1968	98.75	3	5
1970	96.93	7	12
1972	96.58	13	13
1974	89.50	8	40
1976	96.50	3	13
1978	94.95	5	19
1980	92.09	5	31

*Source: Compiled by the author from Congressional Quarterly Service sources.

tremendous advantage in part, at least, because of the weakness of those challenging them (Jacobson, 1981). Table 2.4 dramatizes that situation. For some time political scientists have been noting that an extremely high percentage of these incumbents seeking reelection are in fact reelected. In part we find that this is because few are challenged at all at the first step in the electoral process. In 1978, forty-three members of Congress were reelected with a free ride, no competition in either the primary or the general election. Another seventeen, all Democrats, were challenged in the primary but not in the general. These members are not randomly distributed throughout the country. They tend to come from strong one-party districts. For Democrats, these districts are still concentrated in the South — five in Georgia, four in Florida, three in Alabama, two each in Arkansas and Kentucky. For Republicans, as would be expected, the one-party districts tend to be in the Midwest. More than twice as many Democratic candidates did not face Republican opposition in November as vice versa. Two-hundred and four other members won renomination without competition and then went on to win their November elections. One hundred and thirty-four of these elections were contested against one hundred thirty-four opponents who themselves had been nominated without having to face contested primaries. In the other seventy districts, the opponents had had to win primaries, beating 109 challengers in the process (refer to table 1.1).

One could argue that an ideal democratic model of congressional elections in a two-party system could call for three elections in each district, a contested primary in each party and another choice in November. In those districts in which incumbents sought reelection in 1978, no contested elections were held in 43, one in 152, two in 132, and three in only 48.

On the other hand, in those seats in which members of the Ninety-fifth Congress were not seeking reelection, much more competition was in evidence. Fifty of the fifty-eight new members elected in those open seats faced primary competition; thirty-five of the losers in these races also had primaries. The fields in these primaries were quite large. For example, eight Democrats entered the primary to succeed Yvonne Braithwaite Burke in California's Twenty-eighth District; five Democrats and five Republicans sought their party's nomination in New York's First District, a seat previously held by Otis Pike; and eleven Democrats and four Republicans and eleven Democrats and five Republicans, respectively, entered primaries in open seats in western Pennyslvania's Twenty-first and Twenty-fifth districts. In all, 333 candidates entered contested primaries in these districts; only 27 nominations were decided without primary contests.

Individuals made decisions to run or not to run for a wide variety of reasons. One recurring reason seems to be that it is difficult to challenge an incumbent successfully. When one unsuccessful candidate in an open seat was asked if he would try again, he replied: "Incumbency is always an advantage. For a black, it is almost an invincible asset. I think he's in now for as long as he wants that seat." Another primary loser came to a similar conclusion: "I might try again. We'll have to see. But Bailey is already off and running. It's incredible how they use that office to keep their name in the public eye. It'll be tough."

If one's goal is electoral success, it is not rational to challenge an incumbent. Only five incumbents lost primaries in 1978. Four of the five who beat incumbents in 1978 went on to win general elections.[2] All of these victories were considered upsets, even by the winning candidate. The comments of Congressman Mike Synar, who beat Ted Risenhoover, are typical: "Everyone tried to talk me out of running, even my campaign manager. . . . My last poll showed me losing by almost two-to-one. . . . My top nonfamily advisers all said I should get out of the campaign with grace." But while conventional wisdom said that incumbents could not be beaten in primaries, these candidates all had personal faith in their efforts. Synar continued: "That was the political analysis, but personally I'd talked to over 3,000 people and I never thought I'd lose to him. The family supported me 100 percent and we went in big [in terms of financial commitment]."

2. What follows draws heavily on Maisel, 1981.

All the faith in the world is not enough to beat incumbents in primaries unless many other factors fall into place. One key factor seems to be a small primary field. In each case where an incumbent lost a primary, he was faced with one principal challenger. In two of the races, Synar's victory over Risenhoover and Martin Frost's over Dale Milford in Texas's Twenty-fourth District, only one person took on the incumbent. In two other races there was a third candidate who polled very few votes.[3] In Texas's Fourteenth District, the third candidate polled 20 percent of the votes, while State Representative Joe Wyatt led incumbent Congressman John Young by fewer than 4,000 votes. Texas law requires a majority to nominate, however. Wyatt beat Young handily in the two-person runoff.[4] Mike Synar clearly feels the need for a small primary field if an incumbent is to beaten: "You can't beat an incumbent unless you go at him one-on-one. That was the biggest thing we had to have. I had to keep the field down. In the beginning my name identification was less than 5 percent. That meant we couldn't afford to get lost in an eight-man field."

A small field stands as a necessary condition to beat an incumbent in a primary, but certainly more is needed. Martin Frost pointed out that the incumbent must play a large role in beating himself: "If he'd been reasonably competent, I couldn't have beaten him, even though he wasn't bright or able. But he was not active, he wasn't visible. And when he was visible, he was always quoted as saying some dumb thing. There is no question that he was out of sync with the district and that he wasn't able, but there was still a question of whether he could be defeated. Eventually he just blew it off."

These conditions alone still are not sufficient. However, if the incumbent is "ripe for plucking" and the right challenger can oppose him in a two-person race, an upset could result. Other factors must be present as well, such as money. One cannot claim that a certain amount of money is necessary, because the typical amount spent in different districts varies tremendously, from a few thousand dollars to hundreds of thousands. However, òne can say that a successful challenger must be able to spend enough money to run a campaign comparable to the incumbent's according to the norms of the district. This finding is similar to that which Jacobson (1980) found for general elections. Beyond that, to beat an incumbent, a primary challenger needs to pursue a strategy aimed at exploiting the incumbent's weakness, not necessarily the challenger's

---

3. Tom Easterly defeated incumbent John Breckinridge in Kentucky's Sixth District by 508 votes. A third candidate nearly held the balance despite drawing only 414 votes. In the Second District of Pennsylvania, William Gray won decisively over incumbent Robert Nix. In that race, the third candidate had only 1,500 votes out of over 58,000 cast.

4. As with many other cases in 1978, Young's loss has been atrributed to his personal legal problems, not to further-reaching political trends.

Table 2.5 **New Members' Routes to Election**

| | NEW MEMBER BEAT INCUMBENT | | OPEN SEAT* | |
	Democrats	*Republicans*	*Democrats*	*Republicans*
New Member had Primary	4	10	34	16
New Member had no Contested Primary	1	4	3**	5**
N =	5	14	37	21

(N = 77)

*This table includes the four Democrats who beat Democratic incumbents in primaries and then won election, and the one Republican who won the seat from a Democrat who had beaten an incumbent in a primary, only to lose the general election.
**These numbers include two Democrats and one Republican who were nominated by party committees to fill nomination vacancies caused by death. In each case an incumbent had been nominated for reelection without opposition but had died between the time of nomination and the November election. The Republican total also includes one candidate nominated by party committee when the original nominee resigned.

strengths, and he needs luck. Frost summed up his views succinctly: "I told my campaign manager that even with everything going for us we couldn't make any mistakes and still hope to win. You must have money and spend it right for the district, and you must be lucky."

None of those involved in primaries in which incumbents lost felt that differences on issues was an important factor. Personalities were factors; corruption was a factor; age may have been a factor; but not issues. Not only were issues not a factor in determining the outcome of these primaries, but they were rarely a factor in candidates' decisions to run. Only 14.3 percent of the Democrats and 16.7 percent of the Republicans challenging incumbents stated that issue differences were why they decided to run. There is no evidence that the electorate viewed issue positions as important in primaries either.

While only four new members of the Ninety-sixth Congress won their seats by upsetting incumbents in primaries, nineteen beat sitting members in the general election. Table 2.5 presents information on the route to election followed by these new members of the Ninety-sixth Congress as well as on those who won in open seats.

This table does not include separate cells for the new members who had no general election opponent. Those cells were eliminated because only two new members (Mickey Leland of Texas and Julian Dixon of California) were elected without major-party opposition. Leland won the Democratic nomination in his Houston district by polling nearly 50 percent of the total vote in a seven-person race and then easily winning a runoff. Dixon won his nomination with 48 percent of the vote in an eight-person field; California law allows for nomination by plurality. All seventy-five of the other new members had to win November elections. Sixty-two of them also had to win primary elections.

It is instructive to determine what factors distinguished the 19 races in which sitting incumbents were beaten from the 352 races in which incumbents won reelection. Six of the nineteen incumbents who lost had survived difficult primaries before their November reelection bids. Four of these were members whose reputations had recently been tainted by scandal — Burke of Florida, Carney of Ohio, Eilberg of Pennsylvania, and McFall of California. In these cases it could be argued that the incumbents fell to a heavy one-two combination. None of the eventual winners had difficult nomination contests. State Senator Charles Dougherty ran unopposed in suburban Philadelphia, while the other three winners had primary contests that honed their campaign organizations without causing intraparty schisms. While this hypothesis is appealing, countervailing evidence calls it into question. Other members also touched by scandal — Diggs of Michigan, Flood of Pennsylvania, and Patten of New Jersey, as examples — all survived both primary battles and general-election contests against candidates who should have been able to unify the opposition. The nature of the campaigns and the personal appeal of the incumbents undoubtedly account for the differing results despite similar circumstances (see Johnson and Gibson, 1974; Hacker, 1965).

Table 2.5 also reveals that fourteen of the nineteen who beat incumbents won primary campaigns to gain their party's nomination. Two competing theories purport to explain the relationship between primaries and subsequent general elections. One holds that a candidate try not to split the party in a primary if he or she wants to have any chance to beat an incumbent in November. One primary winner who lost to an incumbent in November commented: "It wasn't a divisive primary, but even though it wasn't, it is difficult to meld different organizations together. This is a problem even with velvet-glove primaries. People get too invested." That winner resented that he did not get more help from his opponents' supporters. He might have felt even more strongly that primaries can hurt the general-election campaign if this primary loser had been his opponent: "I don't go just for the party. That son of a bitch beat me and I'm damned if I was going to turn around and say 'Hurrah for all Democrats.' There's too much in a campaign."

If resentment persists after a primary, then the primary victory might well have been Pyrrhic. However, the second hypothesis predicts that a challenger can benefit greatly from a primary if he or she intends to defeat an incumbent. Two other primary losers supported this view:

> Our primary had a positive effect on Crane. He had to organize more and work harder because he was seriously challenged. Of course, I supported him in the general.

The primary gave Aronoff more name recognition than he'd ever had in his life. It really helped him, gave him a chance.

Name recognition, a good campaign organization, and hard work are certainly important if one is to defeat an incumbent. A nondivisive primary can make a positive contribution to these, but the evidence is clear that such a primary is neither necessary nor sufficient for a challenger's successful effort. As with many other aspects of this study, it appears that individual differences in the context of campaigns account for the differing results.

Ron Paul's victory over Bob Gammage in the Twenty-second District in Texas illustrates the complexity involved in analyzing an election. First, the Paul-Gammage race was a rerun. Repeat contests, particularly after close elections, are common; they account for a high percentage of incumbent losses. Second, the district is highly competitive. Like Illinois's Tenth District, represented until his judicial appointment by Abner Mikva, Paul's district can swing from one party to the other because the parties are of nearly equal strength, and a small vote swing can unseat an incumbent. Third, close House elections are often determined by factors extraneous to the district. Gammage's assessment of his loss was simple: "I think Krueger had Tower beat, but I know I had Paul beat, except for the Clements-Hill thing. Hill did not warm up the minorities. Congressional races and legislative races can't stimulate the emotions; they can't get the minorities out to vote and that's what Democrats need to win here. . . . I probably did more casework than any other district in Texas, but Clements knocked me off; he knocked Krueger off; and he damn near took Jim Maddox too."

While it is not possible to specify all of the factors that lead to incumbents being defeated, local politicians seem to have an intuitive sense of when such a defeat is possible, or perhaps more accurately when it is impossible. When local politicians view an incumbent as truly unbeatable, candidates are less likely to contest nominations.[5] Thus, incumbents sought reelection in 136 of the 140 districts in which neither party had a contested primary in 1978; all but two of those incumbents won. In three of the four seats in this group in which incumbents were not winners, party committees named the nominee to replace a member who had died between the original nomination and the general election, and those nominees won. The political judgment that it made little sense to contest these nominations seems to have been valid.

Jacobson (1981), Abramowitz (1981), and others have looked not at

---

5. Again, this conclusion closely parallels Jacobson's (1980) finding that a challenger's ability to attract financial contributions is a sign that an incumbent is in trouble rather than a cause of that trouble.

those who beat incumbents but at the incumbents who won reelection. Their conclusion seems to be that incumbents have won not only because of their advantages, but also because of the weaknesses of their challengers. This conclusion leads to the final aspect of this view of the decision to seek office: why do others decide not to seek office?

This discussion has not focused on the personal and/or family considerations that go into the decision to enter congressional primaries. Cooper and West (1980) have begun the examination of why more members of Congress retired voluntarily during the decade of the 1970s than in previous years. They have concluded that personal considerations have weighed heavily in those decisions. Because of changes in the job of the congressman — longer sessions, more frequent trips to the district, more disclosure of personal finances, more limitations on acceptable means of supporting income, greater expectations of availability by constituents, and so forth — the job has become less appealing. The same factors have led fewer qualified individuals to seek office as well.

Personal considerations certainly weighed heavily in my decisionmaking process. I made my decision to run for Congress at a time when I was working in Washington and commuting back and forth to Maine on weekends. My children were five and six at the time. I thought long and hard about what a campaign — and even potential service in Congress — would mean to them.

I thought a good deal about the 1976 campaign. When it was clear that seven male candidates were seeking the Democratic nomination that year, a number of us tried to convince Roberta Weil — a talented woman who had served as commissioner of business regulation in Maine and had resigned in protest at the start of the Longley administration when the new governor asked all commissioners for undated letters of resignation — to seek the nomination. We were convinced that a well-known woman could distinguish herself in a crowded field and win the nomination. We were also convinced that Weil had a good chance to defeat Dave Emery. After a series of exploratory meetings, we convinced her that our analysis was correct. Then she decided not to seek the nomination.

Roberta Weil is not only a knowledgeable political activist in her own right, she is also the wife of Gordon Weil. She had lived and worked in Washington when her husband was on Senator McGovern's staff. She knew what the life of a candidate was like. Even though she was convinced that she had a reasonable chance of winning a seat in the Congress, she decided that that life was not for her; she wanted to contribute to the government and to our society, but in a less personally consuming way.

My reasons for moving to Maine from Washington originally were similar to the Weils'. I wanted to live, work, and raise my family in a less pressured atmosphere. I had to decide whether I would give that up for a shot at a life-long ambition. Clearly the goals were conflicting. My family and friends were very supportive; they all pointed out the problems, but they also knew that I would never be happy if I did not take my one good shot.

My personal decision was reached through the ultimate compromise. I rationalized that my children would be proud to have their father in Congress. I vowed that I would not exploit them, but that I would involve them in what I was doing in ways that would be fun for them. I pledged that I would not totally subrogate my family responsibilities and concerns to my political ambition, that I would come home every night during the campaign, that I would go to their school functions, that I would campaign on a theme that one could and should be a good family person if one was to be a good member of Congress.

Oh the hyprocrisy of it all! Candidacy for office and holding office are full-time jobs; one needs the support of family and friends, and one must recognize that those people, those most dear to a candidate, will be placed in intolerable situations. It cannot be avoided. I needed people not only supporting me but also giving up large amounts of their own time, of themselves, for me. I kept saying I would not ask for that and would respect my friends' desires to stay out of politics. I did not ask for it, but I knew I resented it when I did not get it without asking. My worse feelings about my own political experience relate to what kind of person I felt myself becoming — demanding, self-serving, even more egocentric than before.

Until well into his third term David Emery was a bachelor. I argued that only one with family responsibilities can understand the problems felt by our citizens, the problem of feeding a family, preparing for future expenses, worrying about the world we are leaving as our legacy. I was right. But I also feel that it is nearly impossible for one who really cares about his or her family to seek high public office and to serve. Look at the personal problems faced by public officials and members of their families. Ask those familiar with the Washington scene how many "normal" families they can point to. The examples are so few that they stand out from the crowd.

Most of those who seek office do so with the support of their family and friends. About three-quarters of those responding to my questionnaire said their families and friends were encouraging, many enthusiastically encouraging. However, almost half said that at the end of the campaign the personal costs were too high, that they would not seek public office again. One bachelor candidate commented that the campaign was a good experience for him but that: "If I had to settle down, I wouldn't get involved in all of this. It's no way to raise a family. I wouldn't want a wife

Table 2.6 **Local Party Support for Primary Candidates**

LOCAL PARTY SUPPORT*	Total	Open Seat Won	Open Seat Lost	To Challenge Incumbent in Other Party Won	To Challenge Incumbent in Other Party Lost	Against Incumbent in Own Party Won	Against Incumbent in Own Party Lost
Formal	6.9%	30.0%	0	21.4%	6.5%	0	0
Yes, Not Formal	10.2%	20.0%	7.4%	21.4%	10.4%	0	2.1%
Divided	14.7%	10.0%	20.6%	9.5%	15.6%	0	10.4%
Organization Neutral	20.8%	30.0%	20.6%	33.3%	20.8%	0	8.3%
No, Supported Opponent	44.1%	0	47.1%	14.3%	41.6%	0	79.2%
No Organization	3.3%	10.0%	4.4%***	0***	5.2%***	0	0
N =	245	10	68	42	77	0	48

(N = 245)
*See question III.1 on the questionnaire in appendix I for the exact wording of the question and answers.
**See note with table 2.1.
***Percentages do not total 100 because of rounding.

and kids to be shipped off to Washington. It could ruin a family. There is no life there. I'm carefree now, but we'll have to see in the future."

The decision to run is the most complex and important part of the electoral process. Much more needs to be known about why those who run do run and why others do not.

Nearly half of those responding to my questionnaire had held elective political office prior to their 1978 campaigns. Many of those had held either elective or appointive local office (48 percent); 31 percent had been either state representatives or state senators. Approximately one quarter of those entering the 1978 primaries had run for Congress before, two-thirds of those in 1976 but others on many previous occasions.

However, it is important to keep in mind what this previous political experience means. These candidates, by and large, were not well-known leaders of their communities. They were low-level politicos. They were "caught up in" politics, but they had not achieved noteworthy success. Local officials had some advantages over those who had not previously sought office; for instance, they had some name recognition and perhaps some organization in their own areas. Those who had run before had an experience to build on. But basically none of these had tremendous advantages. They were only slightly better off than the other half of the candidates who were novices entering congressional primaries as their first political experience. Most of the losers — and most of the winners — were obscure figures in their communities, known perhaps to other politicians but to few others, looking for lightning to strike to single them out from the masses laboring in political obscurity.

Only 30 percent of those entering these primaries did so with any encouragement from local party officials. As table 2.6 reveals, those who had formal party endorsements (only 6.9 percent) were much more likely to be successful than were other candidates. However, it is equally important to note that party organizations did not become involved at all in most primaries, neither by remaining neutral nor by dividing allegiance among candidates. Further, 44.1 percent ran against the expressed opposition of party people. To some extent this finding is a comment on the state of local party organization at the congressional-district level (see Olson, 1978). But it also raises the question of who encouraged these individuals to run. Few of these candidates win nomination. Even fewer of those who win nomination go on to achieve election. But they do draw votes; at times they affect the outcome of a primary election. They often create crowded primary fields that confuse the electoral process for those voting. Their campaigns have a significant impact on the entire process. Thus, even the campaigns of those who run poorly, without political support, merit closer examination.

The decision to run obviously structures everything else that goes on in the primary process. Who runs, who does not run, how many candidates run. These questions set the stage for the campaigns themselves. Decisions on running are made for a wide variety of reasons, some political, some personal, some rational, some emotional. They are decisions made by individuals pursuing their own goals as they have defined them. But cumulatively they have an important impact on congressional elections in various districts and throughout the nation; and these campaigns in turn have a significant impact on the composition and functioning of the Congress in subsequent years.

3.
CAMPAIGN STRUCTURE AND ORGANIZATION

The commitment to run for office is largely an emotional one. Actually running a campaign involves a series of specific, logistical decisions. It seems that many feel that a great weight is removed once the decision to run is made. They then relax and expect the campaigns to run themselves. In the British tradition of "standing" for office, these candidates expect the mere announcement of their candidacy to be enough to bring forth a groundswell of support that will inevitably lead to anointment as nominee and winner. In American politics there is a name for candidates who follow this route: losers.

Serious candidates must realize that the groundwork for a campaign must be carefully laid before the actual campaign begins. Candidates should, though many do not, do a good bit of research before they decide to run. If they are to be successful, candidates must work hard on structuring an organization. As with so many other aspects of this subject, no one pattern describes all congressional campaign organizations. In this chapter we will see the variety of means employed and identify factors that lead to this variety.

An old political adage holds that any candidate who runs his or her own campaign has a fool as a campaign manager. In Maine's gubernatorial campaign in 1974 I witnessed George Mitchell, who knows as much about the nuts and bolts of politics as anyone and who successfully managed a statewide campaign for Edmund S. Muskie, fall prey to that most common trap. While Anthony Buxton was his campaign manager on paper, Mitchell in fact made all of the decisions and involved himself in decisions about even the minutest detail. I saw the problems caused by a candidate's involvement in the details of campaign management and vowed not to repeat Mitchell's mistake. Then I repeated it.

In retrospect it is clear to me that finding a suitable campaign manager is the most difficult problem faced by a candidate in a congressional (and perhaps any other) primary. No one cares as much about the campaign as does the candidate. Only in unusual circumstances is there a constituency that cares deeply enough about a congressional primary to excite political activists to take on such a race as a *cause célèbre*. If that situation does not exist, the candidate must find a campaign manager who is willing to give up a significant amount of time and to invest a great deal of psychic energy to feed another person's political ambition. Who would make such a sacrifice?

The first group of people who would do such a thing are professional campaign consultants. For some primaries this route is the appropriate one to follow. However, relatively few primaries operate on a budget that permits retaining a campaign professional for the entire length of a campaign. As will be discussed below, money is often a scarce resource in a primary. The candidate and those who share in decisionmaking must determine how much of that scarce resource can or should be allocated to this one position. But even if money is available, questions remain about hiring a professional manager. The main question, beyond which many never get, is whether such a person will have the personal, emotional commitment necessary to subjugate his or her own needs to those of the candidate for the period of the campaign. The tie binding the candidate and the campaign manager must be a terribly strong one. The candidate must know instinctively that the manager is always acting in the candidate's best interest. This trust must be instinctive. It is difficult to have such trust when the campaign manager's motive seems to be financial, not personal.

Therein lies the problem. Few serious candidates find it difficult to attract campaign workers. Many people remain interested in politics. In my own case, I found a large number of my students and former students and many of my friends ready and eager to help. Most were prepared to take on specific assignments and specific responsibilities, even onerous and time-consuming ones. But it was most difficult to find the one person who would assume command, the one person in whom I had implicit faith, who was as knowledgeable about politics as I was (so I did not impose myself into all decision-making), who was committed to the importance of my candidacy, who had essentially unlimited time available, and who did not require more than subsistence wages. Even with two years intervening, the agony I went through in searching for such a person is fresh in my mind.

The most successful choices as campaign managers seem to be family members or close personal friends. Despite the fact that I have been involved in politics all of my adult life, I found, somewhat to my own surprise, that my closest personal friends were essentially apolitical. My family is not a political family. For many reasons I feel it healthy to separate personal and political life, but in selecting a campaign manager, this became a serious problem.

My first attempt to solve this problem was to seek the aid of Pat Ryan, a knowledgeable woman who had been active in the Maine Women's Political Caucus since its inception. She and I agreed that my commitment on women's issues was such that I would be the logical candidate for most of her political associates to support. We attempted to define responsibilities, time commitment, and salary. After a time it became clear that while she was politically committed to my candidacy and certainly had the ability to run a campaign, she did not have the personal commitment needed to devote herself to my effort. That realization did not come easily.

Like many candidates faced with a serious problem, I tried to pipedream the problem away. For more than a month in the early fall of 1977, I proceeded as if my campaign-manager problem was solved. I knew the organization work was not getting done; however, I managed to convince myself that somehow it would all work out. I rationalized that we were in a transition period. A good deal of time was wasted before those working with me became convinced that my campaign management problem not only was not solved, but it had in fact been exacerbated by the passage of time. Even more time ensued before they convinced me of that fact. It is difficult for a candidate to overcome blindness at times.

Eventually I realized that Susan Kenyon, a student of mine whose assigned task was to be head of student volunteers, was performing the job of campaign manager. She and I decided that we should acknowledge this situation and give her the authority necessary to handle the responsibilities she had assumed. We made this decision recognizing that it would cause serious problems. Susan was a college student; she was not a native of Maine; she lacked experience both in terms of campaign management and in terms of knowing the district. Those problems accentuated those already evident in my candidacy. All of those involved in my campaign were aware of that.

However, as a campaign manager Susan also had important positive

Table 3.1 **Difficulty in Finding a Campaign Manager**

DIFFICULTY IN FINDING A CAMPAIGN MANAGER*	Total	Open Seat		To Challenge Incumbent in Other Party		Against Incumbent in Own Party	
		Won	Lost	Won	Lost	Won	Lost
Serious Problem	30.7%	20.0%	26.9%	41.9%	35.1%	0	21.7%
Fairly Difficult	19.7%	40.0%	22.4%	18.6%	15.6%	0	19.6%
Slightly Difficult	11.5%	10.0%	6.0%	11.6%	14.3%	0	15.2%
No Problem	34.4%	20.0%	41.8%	23.3%	31.2%	0	41.3%
None of the Above Marked	3.7%	10.0%	3.0%***	4.7%***	3.9%***	0	2.2%
N =	243	10	67	43	77	0	46

(N = 243)

*See question III.13.d on the questionnaire in appendix I for the exact wording of the question and answers.

**See note with table 2.1.

***Percentages do not total 100 because of rounding.

traits. First and foremost, she was totally dedicated to my candidacy, believing, I think, that our political system needed to attract dedicated idealists. Beyond that, she was smart, energetic, and organized. She had uncanny political instincts and an incredible ability to relate to the entire range of people involved in my campaign — her fellow students, my friends and family, and the whole spectrum of Maine politicians; and she related to them in a way that combined friendship with both deference and respect, drawing from each person the maximum amount he or she could and would give to the campaign, stretching workers to their limit without ever alienating them. My designation of Susan Kenyon as campaign manager, despite all of the problems it entailed, was the wisest decision I made in the entire campaign.

I have discussed my selection of a campaign manager at such length for a number of reasons. First, that choice is the most difficult any candidate makes. Only the lucky few start with the right person in place. As one candidate frustrated in the search for a campaign manager commented, "You have to find someone you respect and you trust and there aren't many of them around"' Nearly a third of those responding to my questionnaire felt that finding a campaign manager was a serious problem for them. Approximately two-thirds answered that designating a campaign head caused some difficulty. Interestingly, those who lost primary campaigns had less of a problem in finding campaign managers than did those who won, and those who spent the least money did not seem to have

Table 3.2 **The Relationship Between the Cost of the Campaign and the Difficulty in Finding a Campaign Manager**

DIFFICULTY IN FINDING A CAMPAIGN MANAGER*	COST OF CAMPAIGN** (in Thousands of Dollars)					
	0-5	6-25	26-50	51-100	101-200	Over 200
Serious Problem	27.7%	27.1%	44.4%	32.3%	27.8%	25.0%
Fairly Difficult	12.8%	20.3%	19.4%	32.3%	27.8%	50.0%
Slightly Difficult	11.7%	8.5%	11.1%	9.7%	22.2%	25.0%
No Problem	41.5%	44.1%	22.2%	22.6%	22.2%	0
None of the Above Marked	6.4%***	0	2.8%***	3.2%***	0	0
N =	94	59	36	31	18	4

(N = 242)

*See question III.13.d on the questionnaire in appendix I for the exact wording of the question and answers.

**Campaign expenditure figures for this and subsequent tables are derived from responses to questions in Part II of my questionnaire. FEC data were not used because it proved impossible to separate primary from general election expenditures for those who won primary elections. These estimates of expenditures on the questionnaire do not appear to be out of line with FEC data on primary losers; thus I have used the data from respondents with some confidence.

***Percentages do not total 100 because of rounding.

much more difficulty than those spending more. The data do not suggest ready explanations for the lack of differences noted. One possible hypothesis is that losers and those with very low budgets do not realize how critical the choice of a campaign manager is and consequently were not troubled by their choice. We do know that many in these categories managed their own campaigns. However, this hypothesis cannot be tested with the information available.

A second reason for the emphasis on how a campaign manager is selected is that it typifies decisionmaking during a campaign. When the candidate is involved in a decision that is either complex or unpleasant or both, he or she frequently puts off making that decision, rationalizes away the necessity for decisions, or gives other (more pleasant) activities a higher priority. Certainly I was guilty of all of the above, and my campaign effort suffered as a consequence. This decision has to be made by the candidate, but the process involved illustrates the need for someone else to run the campaign and to make subsequent decisions of this magnitude.

In addition, the selection of any campaign manager illustrates that much that goes on in congressional primaries involves trial and error and learning by experience (compare Kayden, 1978: chapters 4 and 5). Few people come ready trained with the experience to run a major campaign. Even fewer of those with the experience have the personal rapport with the candidate necessary to form a good team. In my case (and in the cases of many of those I interviewed), I listed the qualities I needed in a campaign manager and sought the perfect person. While I was failing in this search, the campaign went on and my campaign manager emerged as the person who saw what jobs had to be done and did them. The same phenomenon was repeated over and over throughout my campaign.

Congressional campaigns, particularly primaries, are at a strange level in politics. The districts are large in terms of population and often in terms of geographic territory. The office is prestigious. Yet the Congress is removed from the constituency, both physically and often psychologically. Incumbents work hard to build up a rapport with their district (Fenno, 1978); but most challengers are unknown in large parts of the district. Few of the campaigns have large enough budgets to be able to afford the full professional staffs now prevalent in gubernatorial and senatorial campaigns, but the campaigns are extensive enough that all of the same campaign functions must be performed. The result is a good deal of trial-and-error work that involves plugging inexperienced people into slots for which they have shown an aptitude. Organization built in this way proves frustrating for those with considerable campaign experience but highly exciting for those in a campaign for the first time.[1]

How one structures a campaign organization depends on a number of variables relating to the characteristics of the district, the candidate's strengths and weaknesses, and the candidate's resources. As was the case with the selection of a campaign manager, the factors I had to consider in deciding how to structure my campaign are illustrative of those faced by primary candidates throughout the nation.

First, I had to take into account the physical nature of Maine's First Congressional District. The district is geographically large, stretching nearly 150 miles in length and over 50 miles in width. The population is spread throughout the district; while nearly 40 percent of the Democrats live in the Greater Portland area, the others are in smaller cities from Sanford in the south to Waterville in the north, or in rural areas, throughout the district but particulaly along Maine's scenic coast. Politically the Democratic Party is organized on the town (or city) level, and then on the county level. There are nearly two hundred towns and seven counties in the district. The four coastal counties, while the least populous, are in many ways the most active politically.

Unfortunately, my initial strength was concentrated in the northern end of the district. My political base was in the northern part of Kennebec County, where only about 15 percent of the likely voters lived. This was the area in which I was best known and in which I could put together the tightest organization. Only one of my opponents ever made organiza-

---

1. Again, it is evident that the experience in congressional primary campaigns is similar to what Kayden (1978) found in the three statewide campaigns she was examining.

tional inroads into this area, though all three campaigned heavily seeking support.

My strength became progressively weaker as I went further south. I was well known in the southern part of Kennebec County, but so were the other three as they had all worked or lived in the Augusta area, the seat of the state government. Along the coast I was not well known, but I was able to develop organizational support among active Democrats. In the Portland area, Dick Spencer and John Quinn were each better known and each had large cadres of workers. The two leading gubernatorial candidates in the 1978 Democratic primary, Joseph Brennan and Philip Merrill, were each from Portland and had extremely strong campaigns in that area. Quinn was able to piggyback with Joe Brennan, drawing on much of the same Irish strength from the areas in which they grew up; similarly, Spencer's organization paralleled Phil Merrill's, particularly in the suburban areas. Certainly most of those working in the campaign were more interested in gubernatorial than congressional politics and no formal alliances were wrought; however, the ties were clear. Finally, although Spencer and I worked hard to make inroads into southernmost York County, that area has always been politically independent from the rest of the district (and state). York County politics has always been characterized by open intraparty warfare, but in statewide races the wounds are healed and those active in politics come together behind their county's candidate, who becomes essentially a favorite son. Typically this leads to a losing effort and post-primary resentment. That pattern was followed in my primary as nearly all York County politicians reneged on previous commitments and supported Guy Marcotte once he declared.

The biggest resource I had when I began my campaign was a corps of dedicated student campaign workers. As I planned my campaign I had visions of Gene McCarthy's legions trooping through the snows of New Hampshire. I spent many hours daydreaming of a catchy phrase for headline writers to grab hold of, though somehow the ethnic implication of Maisel's Minyans seemed more appropriate for Brooklyn than for Maine.

Student volunteers are, in fact, a tremendous resource. They will do tasks ''more experienced'' political activists shy away from. I felt that a door-to-door campaign, with surrogates committed to me personally and to my view of government, could be very effective. When I planned the campaign, and now, I believe that a candidate is better served by volunteers attracted and dedicated to him or her personally than by old-time political workers who gear up for some campaign every two years. This is particularly true in a primary in which the appeal of party loyalty is lacking. It is also particularly true if the candidate wants to control the way the campaign is run throughout an entire district, rather than relying on the "tried and true" and often futile efforts that are traditionally made. I knew that I had to reach beyond the normal Democratic primary voters if I was to win; those active in party affairs would reach those they always reached — and they would be doing it for the gubernatorial primary, not the congressional primary — but my success depended on reaching other voters.

I felt that students could make this difference for me. However, student volunteers do not come without problems. My students attend a private college; many of them are not native Mainers. For students to play an effective role in my campaign, I had to expand that part of my base from Colby to the various campuses of the state university throughout the district. That meant that I had to spend a good deal of time getting other students as interested in my campaign as my own students were; the others did not know me as well as my students did and would not have the access, because of physical proximity, that mine did. Those factors obviously reduced their incentive to become totally committed.

Furthermore, even the most interested college students are restricted in their dedication to a campaign. They are part-time workers, with the cycle of the academic year as one prime limiting factor. As a college professor I was particularly sensitive to other demands on student time— exams, term papers, courses, even vacations. I also knew I was not likely to compete effectively for students' time against less pressing demands — basketball games, fraternity parties, Winter Carnival. Thus, I needed a large number of workers, assuming that few would be making major time commitments throughout my entire campaign. This was a resource that had to be marshalled and used carefully.

Knowing my strengths and weaknesses and those of my base organization, I first tried to expand my organization by hiring a campaign manager with a separate political base. As I have already discussed, this attempt failed. In a further effort to counter problems inherent in my campaign, my campaign manager and I devised a compromise organizational solution, essentially dividing the campaign into two separate structures.

We established a campaign headquarters in Waterville. Despite the fact that Waterville was geographically far from the center of the district, it was my home base and the center of my political support. The basic functional aspects of the campaign — scheduling, research, writing, press relations, fundraising, media advertising, and the like — were carried out from this headquarters. Most of the work was done by students or former students, working for little or no money. Eventually a corps of ten to fifteen dedicated workers emerged, each working "part-time" and when my campaign fit into their other activities, but each spending far more than forty hours a week on the campaign. Their work was supplemented by that of a few professional consultants who advised us on technical aspects of the campaign, particularly polling and the production of campaign literature and media advertisements.

Parallel to this headquarters organization was a geographic field organization spread throughout the district. We made a concerted effort to name a well-known local Democrat as campaign coordinator in each county and in most of the larger cities and towns. We felt it important to emphasize that mine was not a campaign of an out-of-state college professor supported only by out-of-state students. The local coordinators were given the responsibility for assuring that I met the right people in each area, contacted the appropriate media, attended the right events, spoke on the relevant issues. They also advised us on how to make best use of my time in their areas, how to reach the most voters, both regulars and others who might be attracted by my campaign. Our design was to give these coordinators as much responsibility as they would take.

Each local coordinator was assigned one student volunteer as a liaison person. These student liaisons served a number of roles. First, they were "go-fors." They were to do the legwork that the area coordinators could not or would not do, bringing campaign literature to the area, aiding those who were hosting coffees or cocktail parties, advancing my campaign trips into the area, and accompanying me when I was working in their area. Second, these students knew that I had most faith in them. While I wanted a local resident formally in charge, I knew that the dedication of my area coordinators — with some notable exceptions — did not match that of my students. In my mind each student who served as a liaison was actually in charge of an area. Different patterns emerged. In some areas, the local coordinator essentially took over. In others, the student liaison did all of the work. In still others, the two worked closely together as an effective team.

With the advantage of hindsight I have tried to isolate factors that could explain the different patterns that did emerge. Personality obviously was one critical variable. That is also a variable of extremely limited predictive value.

Party activity seems to be another variable. Local party organizations tend to stay neutral in primary campaigns. Where party organizations do become involved, they normally endorse incumbents. Only 7 percent of the nonincumbents who responded to my questionnaire had formal party endorsements; none of those was running against an incumbent. However, over 40 percent of the respondents answered that an opponent had the formal endorsement; nearly all of those were running against incumbents.

A further word on the role of organized political parties is in order here. Political scientists are nearly unanimous in their opinion that parties are declining in strength (see Crotty and Jacobson, 1980). One of the reasons for this decline is that they have lost control of the nominating process. In those areas where the organization has residual strength, party support is still key in primaries. The comments of these candidates, the first from Philadelphia and the second from Cook County, Illinois, are instructive.

Those people in South Philadelphia vote as their leaders tell them. There is nothing you can do.

Where the organization is strong, the endorsement means more. If the captains favor someone who doesn't win the endorsement, they must drop out. . . . Most important is their precinct work. We had the endorsement in three of the five townships. My winning margin in those three was more than in the whole district.

More common, however, are those areas in which party organization is on the decline. In those districts, candidates must consider party regulars, but their support is not determinative. Charlotte Zietlow is typical of candidates who wanted to avoid alienating party regulars: "I worked real hard with the county organizations. They may not help you, but they really can hurt you if they oppose you. They really can. . . . In Terre Haute there are ten or twelve different factions. They're vocal. They play hardball. I worked very hard at staying out of their battles."

Equally typical were those candidates who felt party regulars could be all but ignored: "The party organization wasn't very active. There were no endorsements at the county or district level. Some local committees were active, but, look, the organization as such doesn't really exist here. The party is broke. It only exists on paper."

Further, even if a party organization does exist, many of those people who hold party office feel that they should personally remain neutral in primary campaigns. Others feel that they can become involved, so long as they offer the resources and forums of their organization equally to all candidates. Party workers are legitimately concerned about the ability of the party organization — weak as it may be — to coalesce behind the eventual nominee. However, neutrality of party workers — those most interested and active in politics — causes a problem for primary candidates. If one cannot build an organization for a primary from party workers, then one must build a personal organization, interesting new people in politics and giving them heavy campaign responsibility. Once the primary is over, the candidates find it difficult to "return to the party fold." Often party regulars are integrated only at the fringes of a candidate's organization in the general election. By remaining neutral in primaries, party regulars have lost the opportunity to have influence in the fall campaign, worsening still the problem of perceived weakness from which most party organizations suffer.

In congressional primaries this problem is particularly severe. In Maine the regulars followed one of three courses. A great many assiduously stayed neutral in all primaries. They felt that was the appropriate role given their formal positions. Others in this group stayed neutral in contested primaries, claiming that they were working for Senator Bill Hathaway, the incumbent, who, though unchallenged in a primary, faced a difficult (and eventually losing) campaign against then Congressman Bill Cohen. Hathaway's campaign was barely gearing up during the spring primary; however, any activity for Hathaway gave party workers an excuse to avoid participating in the campaigns of those contesting primaries and thus to avoid alienating others from the senator's campaign.

Another group decided that they would work for one of the gubernatorial candidates, again staying neutral in the congressional primary. Clearly a governor has more to offer local politicians than does a member of Congress. These Democrats tried to avoid alienating any of the congressional candidates because their prime loyalty was to their gubernatorial candidate. The gubernatorial primary was bitterly contested. The experience after the primary, when many who had supported Phil Merrill never were effectively integrated into the Brennan campaign, demonstrates the difficulty that activity in primary contests can cause party organization. Those who became involved in this way were aware of this difficulty. They determined, however, that loyalty to a gubernatorial candidate — commitment because of personal reasons, ideological reasons, or because of a judgment that one candidate or the other was more likely to be successful in the fall — was more important than remaining neutral to avoid alienation after the primary.

The third group of party regulars — by far the smallest group — became involved in both gubernatorial and congressional primaries. The Democrats in this group tended to be those who were involved in the gubernatorial race and for whom one of the congressional candidates had a particular appeal. Guy Marcotte drew support from York County Democrats because he was their county's candidate; most of them also were working for Joe Brennan. John Quinn attracted many of the Portland Democrats; Quinn and Brennan shared the same Irish, heavily Democratic Portland heritage. Brennan had been involved in Portland politics for many years; Quinn had never before sought elective office. Brennan's organization drew heavily on those who had long been active in Portland and who had supported him in the past; Quinn attracted support from the same group, though their loyalty to him was less strong. Dick Spencer and Phil Merrill had been among the liberal leaders in the Maine legislature. Each was a lawyer from suburban Portland. Many of those most active in Merrill's campaign were also friends of Spencer. While trying to avoid alienating supporters of the other congressional candidates, these workers aided Spencer whenever they could and clearly favored his candidacy.

The third Democratic candidate for governor was former Waterville

Mayor Richard "Spike" Carey. His candidacy caused me certain specific problems. My judgment was that Carey was going to run a poor third. His campaign had many attractions, but it was poorly financed and poorly organized. I wanted to avoid being lumped with him as an "also-ran" from a remote part of the district. I felt I was particularly vulnerable to this assessment because the media as well as the electorate was centered in the Portland area. However, Carey was — and is — very popular in Waterville. If I created too much distance from him, I risked losing the votes of his supporters in Waterville, a group I was certain would turn out to vote. I was particularly concerned because Carey was as far from me on the ideological spectrum as were any of the candidates; yet I knew many of his supporters would vote for me merely because of the Waterville connection.

Carey and I never explicitly discussed this problem, but it was effectively worked out by our staffs. Those few local Democrats who were friends of both of us worked for both of us, but generally separately. Most of the normal activists worked for one or the other of us. In the Waterville area we concentrated heavily on ensuring a good turnout; we knew this would help both of us without alienating any other candidate's supporters.

Outside of the Waterville area most of the party regulars drawn to my campaign were attracted because of my stands on specific issues. Dick Spencer and I shared views on many issues; John Quinn was perceived as a liberal because of his activities as a consumer advocate, but he had not taken any stand on most issues and seemed to take the politically popular stands on others. Marcotte entered the race hoping to win by espousing the politically popular right-wing positions: anti-abortion, anti-gun control, pro-Proposition 13-type legislation, and so on. Spencer chose not to respond to Marcotte's rhetoric. I chose to attack. Maine's Democratic party is generally thought to be conservative. There are, however, a number of activists who first joined the party during George McGovern's campaign for the presidency and who stayed involved when Mo Udall ran in 1976. Those party regulars who supported my campaign tended to come from this group, no matter which candidate for governor they favored.

One of those interviewed expressed disappointment in the activity of his workers, commenting, "That's what I found out about a lot of liberals. They chant but they won't go out and hustle." In Maine the true ideological liberals are so few that they would not make much noise were they to chant. As a consequence, when they do become involved, they hustle. But liberals in Maine, as in other places, seek purity. And they are individuals with personal allegiances. Some found fault with me; others preferred one of my opponents. However, I was pleased that by running a campaign based on issues I could earn the support and active effort of most in this group.

Chart 3.1 **Maisel for Congress Campaign Organization Chart**

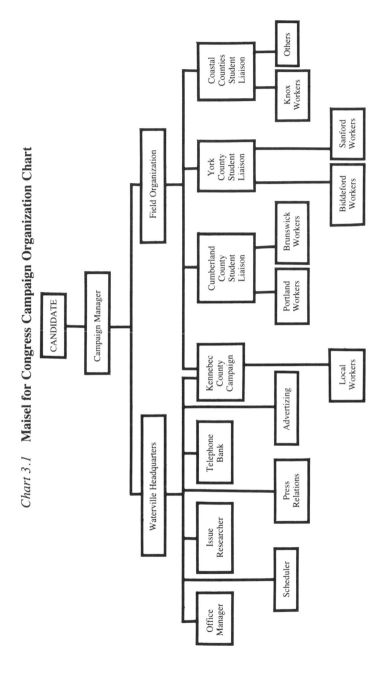

Chart 3.1 shows my campaign organization as it existed on paper. However, no campaign organization of which I am aware has ever worked in fact the way it is laid out on paper. Responsibility and influence flow to those with time and ability. Some do two or three jobs; some jobs do not get done. My campaign was no exception.

I have already mentioned that my campaign manager was one of my students who had started out as the head of my student volunteers. It is instructive to see where the rest of my staff came from. The common thread is a Colby College connection, but each key participant came to the campaign in his or her own way and for his or her own reasons.

Bob Walsh wrote issue papers for me and generally helped with research. A Colby graduate with majors in government and economics, Bob had worked in Washington on the staff of Congressman Norman E. D'Amours (D., N.H.). He came back to New England and volunteered to work for me for room and board. Clearly, he wanted more responsibility than he had been given on Capitol Hill. His services were invaluable to me; he knew Washington issues, controversies, data sources, and the like. During the course of the campaign, he and I prepared major issue papers on nearly every topic current in the Congress. We worked with local experts and drew on our connections in Washington. This aspect of my campaign clearly reached its desired objective; newsmen interviewing me frequently commented on the breadth and depth of my knowledge about the job I sought and the current concerns of the Congress. Bob could not have performed more ably. Had I been successful, he would now be a legislative assistant on the Hill. As it is, he has returned to law school.

Bob worked closely with Bob Duchesne, my press secretary, who was news director at Waterville's local radio station. Bob graduated from Colby in 1975 as a government major. He had worked in radio all through college and hoped my campaign would be his ticket into a better market. Waterville is not the media center of Maine, and Bob knew almost none of the other news directors in the state. Each week he traveled to a different area, meeting newspeople, making contacts, setting up interviews for me. It took him awhile to acclimate to his job, but eventually he and Bob Walsh worked out a system through which we were issuing locally plugged news releases daily to the areas in which I was traveling and more wide-ranging releases three times a week. Of all of the candidates running in both parties for any offices in 1978, only Dick Spencer approached getting as much press coverage as I did. Bob Duchesne learned what it took to have a story carried on the wires and what it took to get news play from stories not on the wire. Another trial-and-error success, Bob did not end up on Capitol Hill, but he is now broadcasting in the Washington area.

All trials by fire did not end up as successes, however. My first scheduler was a very bright young woman who had decided to take a leave from Colby. We gave her a detailed plan outlining how much time each month I wanted to spend in each area, a division arrived at through a careful analysis combining my strength and the potential turnout. We told her when I had to be in Waterville, showed her schedules from other candidates' campaigns, gave her a small salary, a desk, and a telephone, and instructed her to fill my days as full as she could until I complained. For two months no candidate ever had it easier. I could have played golf, taken naps, and perhaps even written this book. I was frustrated, and Susan Kenyon was frustrated; I was not seeing voters; I was not making contact; I was not raising money or making any headway.

Despite my frustration, I did not know what to do about it. I could not face the thought of firing someone I was only paying twenty-five dollars a week. Then one day I walked into the office and Susan told me that Pat Hotchkiss was my new scheduler. My former scheduler was now office manager. I asked her how she had done that. "Well," she said, "someone had to and it was obvious you wouldn't. I gave her a five-dollar raise and told her it was a promotion." That is why a candidate needs a campaign manager.

Suddenly lists began to appear, lists we should have had. We had lists of plants by location, complete with times of shift changes, numbers of workers, names of union leaders; lists of Rotary, Kiwanis, and Lions meetings; lists of high-school civics teachers, bowling leagues, sporting events; and quickly lists of speaking engagements, coffees, and cocktail parties. My days were filled from 6:00 A.M. to 1:00 A. M. Schedules came complete with drivers, meals, sleeping accommodations. I was a candidate in seventh heaven. Pat was also a former student who had left Colby. She had no previous political knowledge and no political ambitions. She was killing time before she went abroad to school. But she had one important asset. She knew how to use the telephone. She checked in daily with local coordinators, read every newspaper in the district, and never was off the telephone. It was as if it was a personal affront to her every time I took a deep breath. She was not often affronted.

We also had favorable and unfavorable experiences with consultants. The first consultant I contacted was Bill Hamilton, a Washington-based pollster. I knew Hamilton from his service as one of the public members of the Obey commission. He is highly respected among union officials and Democratic politicians in Washington. I asked his advice on how to assess my chances in Maine's First District. He convinced me that money spent on early polling, even in a relatively low-cost congressional campaign, was money well spent. He then designed a poll to be administered by volunteers on a door-to-door basis and came to Maine to train students as poll takers. His work was thorough, precise, and timely. Later I will discuss the use of polling in congressional primaries in some detail. For now, let me summarize his findings, based on a poll of a sample drawn from Democrats and some Independents (who can enroll on primary day and vote in Maine's primary) when the only candidates who had filed were Dick Spencer and myself:

> Maisel is not well known in the district, but an issue-oriented campaign could be successful; the primary is winnable, though it will not be easy; but David Emery has the highest positive evaluation of an incumbent ever recorded by Hamilton and Staff among voters in the other party; no strategy for a November election appears feasible.

I decided to run anyway. Here, as so often, the conclusion seemed inevitable: political ambitions often override rational judgment.

When it became clear that my campaign would be run by "amateurs," I decided that it would be wise to hire professional campaign consultants for advice on strategy and particularly media. I discussed the choice of a firm with Democrats I know in Washington and throughout the state. The prestige firms were far beyond my ability to pay. I discussed my campaign with Ad Media, an Augusta advertising firm that had run Governor James Longley's successful campaign in 1974. After a brief discussion, two things were clear to me. First, they had the best track record of any firm in the state. Second, we could not work together; their idea of winning was to create a candidate around popular, "catch" issues. Winning meant nothing to me if I had to violate my political beliefs.

Through a friend in Boston I contacted Caulfield and Associates, a relatively new firm run by Bob Caulfield, who had been active in Massachusetts politics for some time. They claimed that their expertise was media and coordinating a media strategy with the other aspects of campaigning. A long rendition of a painful experience seems superfluous. Suffice it to say that some people are talkers and others are doers. In my opinion listening to Bob Caulfield cost me several thousand dollars that could have been better spent later in the campaign. The "doing" I did in this case was suggesting to Caulfield that the time had come for us to sever our ties. His expertise in Boston did not transfer well to Maine.

Eventually we discarded the idea of hiring a political consultant. A small group of us devised our strategy based on what I had to say and to whom I could appeal. Duffy, Darrow, and Baer, a Camden-based advertising firm without previous political experience, translated our strategy into a media campaign that, while not elegant was more than adequate to get my name known and my message across.

These experiences again point to the difficulties inherent in congressional primaries. Polling and professional advice on strategy, media, and like matters are thought to be essential in candidate-oriented campaigns.

Yet the average amount of money spent in congressional primaries by nonincumbents responding to my questionnaire was only $14,000. Only 8.8 percent spent over $100,000. Money is a scarce resource. If a high percentage of this scarce resource is spent to pay for advisers, little is left to implement their advice. If advisers are not consulted, then the money spent implementing a campaign strategy may be spent ineffectively. As I pondered this dilemma during my campaign, I often thought of Yul Brynner's famous conclusion in *The King and I,* "'Tis a puzzlement!'"

The actual experience of our field organization also differed from that which we plotted on our organizational chart and in our strategic outline. Our goal was to twice contact every home in the district that housed any Democratic voters — once in person and once by telephone — and to make our campaign as visible as possible in as many areas as possible. Carefully compiling voter lists by street, we determined how many volunteer-hours this effort would take. Early on we decided that such an approach in the more rural areas was infeasible and reset our strategy to aim at the 80 percent of the Democratic voters living in more heavily populated parts of the district. Dividing the district geographically, we set specific goals for each of our county and town coordinators.

In some areas the strategy worked perfectly; the goals were matched or exceeded. In other areas any resemblance between our organizational goals and what happened was pure happenstance. Four factors account for the variations in my success in the field in different parts of the district. The first factor was the effectiveness and dedication of my local coordinators. Some, like Sharon Kimball in Brunswick, a woman who had no previous political experience, and Pat Richey, an activist in coastal Knox County, assumed that if we gave them a task it was doable and they simply found a way to do it. Others, typically those with more traditional political backgrounds in larger areas, viewed our tasks as monumental and gave up before they started. The work of my local coordinators covered a spectrum from total dedication and effectiveness to merely allowing us to use a name with no local effort expended.

A related factor was the strength of my opponents and of the gubernatorial candidates in various areas. Door-to-door campaigning requires volunteer hours. Only a certain number of people are interested in politics. Our area coordinators became discouraged when most of the other people they knew were working for other candidates — Marcotte and Brennan in York County, Brennan and Merrill in Portland, Spencer and Merrill in the areas around Portland.

In some of these areas we were able to supplement our local strength with student volunteers. However, our success at doing this varied with a third factor, the distance from Waterville. If a carload of volunteers had to drive two hours to an area and another two hours back, twenty volunteer hours were wasted not contacting voters. As a result, we tended to concentrate student volunteers in areas closest to college campuses. Other areas were consequently ignored.

The fourth factor, referred to earlier, was the periodic nonavailability of our volunteers. Campaign events are planned on a schedule related to local activities and the approach of election day. These relate to the life of college students in a random way. Thus, we could not create the impression of a large-scale organization in an area by ''importing'' workers to a certain event if those workers were not available on the day they were needed. In some areas the local voters assumed my volunteers must be everywhere at all times because we never seemed to miss anything going on in their town. In other areas, because of scheduling problems, the campaign was practically invisible.

Like many other campaigns, mine existed on two levels. Everything looked good on paper. But reality could not match that plan. Few of those working on my campaign were paid. My total ''staff'' payroll for the campaign was under $6,000. Tasks were divided so that each volunteer did what he or she had the time, commitment, and ability to do. Some did a little of everything, pitching in when others let us down, working eighteen-to-twenty-hour days, designing leaflets in the morning, contacting voters in the afternoon, stuffing envelopes in the evening, and greeting the graveyard shift at a factory at night. Others accepted major responsibilities and did little; but their contribution, however small, was appreciated too, for they were giving to me when they could have been spending that same time on their own activities.

These patterns were similar to those of others who ran in congressional primaries. Over a quarter of those who responded to my questionnaire (27.6 percent) served as their own campaign managers. These candidates had difficulties typical of individuals trying to do more than one job. ''I was my own campaign manager and I didn't know anything. I needed a real good man to do the precinct work.'' ''I ran my own campaign. Our problem was that there were four of us who tried to do everything. We did scheduling, mailing, everything right out of this office.'' Only 18.4 percent hired a professional to handle this most important task. Over half chose either a friend (33.2 percent), a business associate (7.2 percent), or a relative (11.2 percent) to direct their efforts. It is probably safe to assume that the candidates themselves were heavily involved in running their campaigns. Table 3.3 shows the relationship between choice of campaign manager and success in primary campaigns. Because of the large number of cells, Ns are small and percentaging might be deceiving. However, the pattern is clear. Those with professionals as campaign managers were most likely to be successful. Those who chose business associates also had a good success rate. Those who

Table 3.3 **Individuals Serving As Campaign Managers**

CAMPAIGN MANAGER						
			TYPE OF CANDIDATE			
		Open Seat	*To Challenge Incumbent in Other Party*		*Against Incumbent in Own Party*	
		Won	*Lost*	*Won*	*Lost*	*Won*	*Lost*
Self		1*	17	7	25	0	19
Relative		0	9	4	10	0	5
Friend		4	26	9	19	0	14
Business Associate		2	6	7	1	0	2
Professional Manager		2	11	15	12	0	5
Other		0	2	0	1	0	3
	N =	9	71	42	68	0	48

(N = 238)
*Cell entries are number of respondents giving each answer.

chose friends or relatives, and especially those who ran their own campaigns, were much less successful. Of course, one cannot infer causality from this analysis. Other factors, money high among them, obviously contributed to both variables.

Most congressional primaries in 1978 were essentially volunteer efforts. Of those responding to my questionnaire, 58.4 percent had no paid staff at all; only 5.6 percent paid more than five people. Those who were paid worked for very low wages; 75 percent of the campaigns had a total weekly payroll that peaked at under $400. On the other hand, 20 percent of the campaigns had more than ten volunteers who worked full-time for over a month; about three-quarters of the campaigns had more than twenty volunteers who worked more than twenty hours a week. Some readers might feel that these numbers of volunteers seem low. Drafting volunteers for a congressional campaign, as I have mentioned, is not easy. Over a fifth of those who responded to my questionnaire (22.4 percent) felt that drafting volunteers was a "serious problem" for their primary campaign; another 31.3 percent felt that finding enough volunteers was "fairly difficult"; only 20.3 percent answered that this aspect of the campaign caused them "no problem at all."

This difficulty is understandable if one recalls where congressional campaigns, particularly primaries, fall in the pecking order of concerns for party campaign workers. Major statewide offices are more important for most of these workers; candidates for governor and United States senator have much less difficulty in attracting the party faithful to their campaigns. The candidates have more of a celebrity status and the offices sought afford more opportunities to reward the faithful.

In addition, local offices also have more attraction to local workers. In those cases the candidates might not be celebrities, but they are personally well known, the "friends and neighbors" attraction applies in only one part of a district as vast as most congressional districts. Furthermore, local party workers frequently aspire to office themselves. Congress seems remote and frightening, beyond the ambition of most. However, local offices are well within their grasps. Working on local campaigns, then, has the attraction of giving valuable experience and of providing the opportunity to win the allegiance of a political friend who may be very helpful in the future.

If one looks beyond regular party workers, the sources of volunteers are less fertile. Some candidates have logical groups to which they can turn. My students were one such group; single-issue candidates have been able to draw from their issue constituency, and so on. One of the fascinating phenomena that I discovered, and one that many whom I interviewed commented upon as well, was how few of my friends were "political." Friends can be extremely loyal and supportive; many of my friends who were lifelong Republicans became Democrats to vote in my primary. But no matter how dedicated and loyal they may be, many nonpolitical people will not engage in certain "political" activities, the prime among these being trying to convince someone else to vote for a particular candidate. With political apathy, no matter how measured, on the rise, the problem of attracting volunteers to campaigns that are largely carried on by volunteers can only become more difficult.

In looking at the full range of primary experiences, one sees that a number of campaigns were not much more than one-person shows. Of those responding, 31.8 percent answered that they had no full-time workers; 27.7 percent said that no one worked as much as twenty hours a week, even during the last month of campaigning. None of these candidates won his or her primary. The experience of Al Vera, who finished far back in the field in the race to succeed Barbara Jordan in Houston, is not at all atypical: "My organization was very meagre. I had one full-time person and then volunteers. Some of the other candidates came up to me to say they were impressed with the quality of my volunteer help, especially because they were so young, my high school students, but we didn't have their numbers." Vera and his volunteers were serious about running for Congress, but they were out of their league. His campaign was one of many in 1978 in which the candidate had no chance of winning but drew enough votes and attention to have an impact on the eventual result.

One of the serious systemic problems that is apparent from an overview of the congressional primary process relates to the number of "nonserious" candidates who win a place on the ballot. These candidates can be identified in many ways — motivation, organizational effort, fund-

Table 3.4 Number of Full-Time Volunteers

FULL-TIME VOLUNTEERS*	Total	Open Seat		To Challenge Incumbent in Other Party		Against Incumbent in Own Party	
		Won	Lost	Won	Lost	Won	Lost
0	32.5%	11.1%	16.7%	30.8%	41.3%	0	46.7%
1-5	34.6%	0	37.9%	35.9%	73.3%	0	31.1%
6-10	13.7%	44.9%	15.2%	15.4%	12.0%	0	6.7%
11-15	4.3%	0	10.6%	0	2.7%	0	2.2%
16-20	2.6%	11.1%	3.0%	2.6%	1.3%	0	2.2%
Above 20	12.4%***	33.3%***	16.7%***	15.4%***	5.3%***	0	11.1%
N =	234	9	66	39	75	0	45

(N = 234)
*See question III.5 on the questionnaire in appendix I for the exact wording of the question and answers.
**See note with table 2.1.
***Percentages do not total 100 because of rounding.

Table 3.5 Number of Volunteers Working Twenty Hours per Week

NUMBER OF VOLUNTEERS*	Total	Open Seat		To Challenge Incumbent in Other Party		Against Incumbent in Own Party	
		Won	Lost	Won	Lost	Won	Lost
0	28.0%	0	20.6%	23.7%	37.3%	0	33.3%
1-10	33.9%	10.0%	33.8%	34.2%	30.7%	0	44.4%
11-20	14.0%	20.0%	9.1%	7.9%	14.7%	0	8.9%
21-50	14.8%	40.0%	17.6%	18.4%	12.0%	0	6.7%
51-100	5.1%	0	2.9%	13.2%	4.0%	0	4.4%
Above 100	4.2%	30.0%	5.8%***	2.6%	1.3%	0	2.2%***
N =	236	10	68	38	75	0	45

(N = 236)
*See question III.6 on the questionnaire in appendix I for the exact wording of the question and answers.
**See note with table 2.1.
***Percentages do not total 100 because of rounding.

raising ability, personal campaign effort — none of which alone is sufficiently rigorous to isolate particular individuals but which together reveal a pattern defining a type of campaign that does not make a serious effort

Table 3.6 Activities Performed by Campaign Organizations

ACTIVITIES			ACTIVITY PERFORMED BY:		
			Candidates and	Candidates and	Not
	Candidate	Paid Staff	Volunteers	Paid Staff	Volunteers	Done
Speech Writing	67.5%*	3.6%	3.6%	6.3%	11.1%	6.7%
Issue Development	43.7%	7.5%	12.7%	6.7%	19.7%	6.7%
Press Relations	40.9%	17.1%	15.5%	8.7%	12.7%	3.6%
Fundraising	31.7%	2.8%	19.4%	3.2%	26.2%	12.7%

(N = 243)
*Cell entries are the percentage who reported that each activity was performed by the specified actors. These responses are derived from answers to questions III.8.c., III.8.d., III.8.e., and III.8.g. in the questionnaire in appendix I.

to attract a plurality of the voters but for one reason or another attracts enough voters to confuse the electoral process. These campaigns appear again and again in this study and will be identified where appropriate.

Tables 3.4 and 3.5 demonstrate that congressional primaries throughout the nation tend to be largely personal and volunteer efforts. Candidates were asked to examine a list of activities normally associated with campaigns and to identify those in their campaigns who had primary responsibility for those activities. Candidates themselves were heavily involved in certain kinds of activities, typically those concerned with presentation of issue positions. Many activities, particularly those involved with contacting the voters, were dominated by volunteers. Professional campaign aides were involved in only a few activities, most frequently advertising and media work. Again, the variety of experiences is instructive. Some of the campaigns undertook few, if any, of the typical activities cited. Other campaigns relied on professionals for almost every aspect of campaigning.

What then can be concluded about the role of campaign organizations in congressional primaries? We hear a great deal about the role of media and the so-called "new politics" in candidate-centered campaigns. Congressional primaries are candidate-centered campaigns. The role of party is minimal. But "new politics," at least to the extent that that term implies media campaigns run by professional consultants without grass-roots organization, is not yet typical of congressional primaries. The scope of the campaign is sufficient to call for such techniques, but the resources available to the candidates are not sufficient to sustain such efforts.

Rather, each congressional candidate mounts a campaign commensurate with the extent of his or her resources. In some cases, as in the $200,000-$300,000 primaries in some Texas districts, the campaign organizations are in every way parallel to those now typical in campaigns for governor or United States senator. Incumbents who face serious challenges are frequently capable of mounting such efforts, particularly if the challengers can raise and/or spend enough money to run such campaigns. But these examples are atypical.

Much more common is the campaign staffed largely by volunteers. Some resources are expended on paid media, but much more is spent on more traditional activities — door-to-door campaigning, telephoning, leaflet drops, mailings. These activities are most frequently carried out by volunteers, campaign workers dedicated to one candidate's effort.

My first experience in electoral politics was as a volunteer worker for a congressional campaign. I was convinced that my candidate's success would make a major difference in the Congress as the issues of war and peace were debated. In that belief I was probably mistaken, but the interest in politics built during that campaign never abated.

I saw the same thing happen to many of the volunteers working on my campaign in 1978. Some caught the political bug, an infection they will never lose. Others were immune. That kind of an organization was one I was comfortable with. I knew what my volunteers were experiencing and could help them relate to that experience. In that way I feel I had an important impact on those working for me. My political organization also had as much impact on the district as my resources would allow. Certainly my organization was not perfect; we made lots of mistakes, but we learned from them and improved.

From looking at organizations throughout the nation, I would conclude that my organization was less professional than some, but better than most. In type, it was similar to many. Candidates assess their resources and set their organizational goals. The resources are not what have been anticipated. The goals are not all met. Volunteers or near-volunteers perform most of the campaign activities. Candidates soon learn that only so much can be done by volunteer labor. Those with the best plans and the strongest commitments put together the best organizations. Such organizations make a big difference in campaigns, but they are only the determining factor if other resources and activities are equal. Next we will turn to an examination of some of these.

4.
FINANCING
THE CAMPAIGN

Before I firmly decided to run, I telephoned Dick Spencer. I was trying to learn something about his intentions. He was probing my ideas as well. Each of us used the pretense that we wanted to keep the lines of communication open, that we wanted to avoid a bitter primary. Each of us really wanted information.

I learned more of substance than Dick did. My ideas were still amorphous; I had little to tell. Dick's campaign was already well thought out, information that frightened me. At one point I asked him what he thought the primary would cost. "About $50,000, more or less."

"That's just about what I'm budgeting, too." I had no idea where I would raise that money or how I would allocate it, but in that brief conversation, nearly a year before the primary, my budget was set. Spencer ended up spending $93,000 in his primary; I spent $52,000, amazingly close to that $50,000 figure arrived at while bluffing on the telephone.

No one doubts the importance of money in today's campaigns. If one has enough to spend, a candidate can do without a large volunteer organization; candidates can "buy" professional organizations or run media campaigns. If a candidate does not have enough to compete with

Table 4.1 **Differences Between Anticipated and Actual Costs of Congressional Primaries**

ACTUAL COST OF CAMPAIGN* (in Thousands of Dollars)	ANTICIPATED COST OF CAMPAIGN** (in Thousands of Dollars)					
	0-5	*6-25*	*26-50*	*51-100*	*101-200*	*Over 200*
0-5	93.8%	35.1%	11.1%	10.4%	16.7%	0
6-25	4.7%	50.9%	37.8%	18.8%	8.3%	0
26-50	1.6%	14.0%	31.1%	18.8%	16.7%	0
51-100	0	0	17.8%	35.4%	16.7%	20.0%
101-200	0	0	2.2%	16.7%	33.3%	20.0%
Over 200	0 ***	0***	0***	0***	8.3%	60.0%
N =	64	57	45	48	24	5

(N = 243)
*See question II.2 on the questionnaire in appendix I for the exact wording of the question and answers.
**See question II.1 on the questionnaire in appendix I for the exact wording of the question and answers.
***Percentages do not total 100 because of rounding.

others running, he or she must offset that disadvantage with other significant resources — volunteers, name recognition, or perhaps a divisive issue. Underfinanced candidates usually lose, no matter what other resources they can muster. This has already been documented for challengers' campaigns against incumbents in general elections (Jacobson, 1980; Maisel and Cooper, 1981); it is equally true in primaries.

Given the importance of money in congressional campaigns, it is amazing that decisions in this area are made with as little hard information and as much uncertainty as are most other judgments in these contests. Candidates make decisions on what a campaign will cost, on how much can be raised, and on how much personal investment will be necessary with an incredible dirth of information.

Table 4.1 shows how far actual campaign expenses varied from what candidates expected their campaigns to cost. With the exception of those expecting to run very inexpensive campaigns (under $5,000), a majority of those responding did not spend what they expected to. Two types of divergence are apparent. Most spent considerably less than they anticipated. Those who expected to spend under $50,000 typically were not able to raise the amount of money they anticipated. A majority of those whose actual expenses exceeded their projections ran more expensive campaigns. These candidates had the ability to raise money or to spend their own money and spent more than they expected as the costs of their campaigns escalated to meet the amount of revenue they could obtain.

Candidates do not enter campaigns without thinking about fundraising. The problem arises in making the conversion from planning what one would like to raise and spend to what is practical. Some clues exist about what a campaign will cost. Since 1974, the Federal Election Commission has maintained records of the amounts raised and spent in federal elections. Any candidate can go back to the previous election and ascertain how much each candidate spent and how that money was spent. That is the kind of research that can be, should be, and usually is done before a campaign starts. Candidates can ascertain not only how much previous campaigns cost, but also how the money was raised and who gave large amounts. These data provide an invaluable starting point as perspective candidates gain information about funding their primaries, but circumstances change between elections.

Of those responding to my questionnaire, 50.6 percent said that more was spent in 1978 by far than had been spent in 1976. Only 8.8 percent answered that more had been spent in 1976. Candidates generally are aware of factors peculiar to one election: a large field, one extremely wealthy candidate, or the like. They also are aware of the general escalation in the cost of campaigning. By looking at previous races, they can find out what range of expenses is involved, from a few thousand dollars in the minority party in some northern districts, to the multi-hundred-thousand-dollar campaigns common in the oil-affected districts of Texas. They also can see how candidates have raised money in the past. The difficulty is matching one's own abilities to raise money with what is known from the past.

In 1976, Rick Barton won the Democratic primary in Maine's First Congressional District, spending $36,000. Runner-up Jim Mitchell spent $25,000; in total $130,000 was spent by the seven-man field. Given the rate of inflation, $50,000 did not seem out of line for my budget, despite the fact it was arrived at through no rational process. The next step was to determine how I was going to raise that money.[1]

My first decision was that I would spend no more than $10,000 of my own money. Every candidate must decide how much he or she is willing to spend or borrow. The difficulty is in enforcing that judgment.

Next I had to determine where else I could turn for money, sources that were uniquely mine. Barton had raised a good deal from family; Spencer also had personal and family wealth. Unfortunately, I could not match those sources. I knew I could raise money from family and friends in Buffalo. There was an obvious disadvantage to raising money outside of the district. However, I knew I would be dubbed an ''out-of-stater'' anyway. I felt that the negative publicity that might follow from raising money in Buffalo was outweighed by the potential uses of that money, particularly if it was raised early in the campaign. I also knew Spencer

1. The four candidates in Maine's First Congressional District actually spent over $200,000 in 1978.

would raise a good deal of money out-of-state, so, in the two-person field that was emerging, the issue would be defused. Based on guesswork, or rather on what I would need to reach my ultimate goal rather than on what giving potential existed, I set a goal of $10,000 for this effort. I turned to my best childhood friend, Warren Gelman, to reach this goal; though as nonpolitical as any of my friends, he accepted this job and, with my family, eagerly jumped into this most unpleasant part of campaigning.

I hoped I could turn my other political liabilities into financial assets as well. I decided that I would actively solicit my Harvard classmates, Harvard alumni living in Maine, Colby alumni living in Maine, the Colby faculty, my Washington contacts, and Maine's small Jewish community. I consulted friends in each of these groups, seeking their help in gaining financial backing in whatever way seemed most appropriate — personal solicitation, letters, or a combination of each. These friends were enthusiastic in their support and optimistic about the success I would have. Juggling figures to make my goal obtainable, again with little knowledge of actual potential, I set $15,000 as the total to be raised from these groups.

If these goals were met, I would only have to raise $15,000 from traditional Maine sources. Given the spending history of the district but also taking into account that there was to be a hard-fought gubernatorial primary and an expensive senatorial campaign on the horizon, this figure seemed reachable. I sought the help of political friends in Maine who were tuned in to those who normally supported political candidates. I knew what various methods could be used, such as individual solicitations and small or large fundraising events. As was the case when I sought a campaign manager, many said they would help, but no one was willing to take on the responsibility for coordinating the entire effort.

I was fortunate that Jon Eustis, another good friend with no previous political experience, accepted my request for help and volunteered to serve as campaign treasurer. The federal campaign financing reforms put an incredible record-keeping burden on campaign committees. Many candidates had to spend money (which could have been used for more productive campaign purposes) to pay for an accountant to guarantee compliance with FEC regulations. Half of the respondents to my questionnaire claimed that FEC regulations restricted their fundraising efforts. Over three-quarters of those responding answered that FEC reporting requirements caused them some degree of difficulty. Jon relieved me of these burdens. My fundraising effort never did achieve any degree of coordination, but Jon Eustis played two key roles, restricting my personal debt and keeping the FEC off of my back. Anyone who has run for office since the 1974 reforms went into effect can appreciate the extent of the debt I owe him for undertaking that thankless and difficult task.

Anyone familiar with recent campaigns must have heard Hubert Humphrey's lament about having to raise money for campaigns. According to Senator Humphrey, attempting to raise money for a political campaign is a "disgusting, degrading, demeaning experience" (Jacobson, 1980: 170). If anything, Senator Humphrey understated the problem. Nothing is more difficult in a political campaign than raising money. The effort takes an enormous amount of a candidates time and energy. The effort is rarely personally rewarding. But it is absolutely necessary. Individuals do not give money to political campaigns, especially campaigns without high saliency, unless they are asked in a way that is personally meaningful to them. Congressman Mike Synar's comments are typical of many of those I interviewed: "I'm convinced that in a congressional race the candidate has to raise the money himself, only he can do it, no one can successfully do it for him."

My experience certainly confirms that experience. Those who had a personal connection with me, those whom I contacted during the campaign, supported me. In Buffalo we raised $7,500 at a fundraiser I attended. My Colby faculty colleagues gave nearly $3,000, each impressive amounts considering previous political giving by these groups. On the other hand, only those Harvard classmates I personally contacted, those who signed the fundraising letter on my behalf, contributed. If one excludes the contributions of the signatories, that fundraising letter was a fundloser. The same can be said of my appeal to Colby and Harvard alumni in Maine. It is likely that a majority of those receiving those letters were Republicans. They were unconvinced by the logic that, regardless of views on issues, they would be well served by my candidacy. Only those I went to see personally contributed at all.

Perhaps the most sobering experience I had was the realization of how little support I received from the Jewish community. I had the support of Democrats who were leaders in the Jewish community. My appeal was a well-reasoned one, based on my commitment to the State of Israel, Emery's poor record on Israel, and the lack of interest in the Middle East by my primary opponents. The response, again with few exceptions, was full of promises and devoid of fulfillment. Active Democrats pleaded that they did not want to alienate the others should one of my opponents win. Republicans said they would support me in the general election but did not want to be involved in Democratic party affairs. It was clear that my judaism and commitment to Israel hurt me politically; I was frustrated that those who shared my views on these matters did not feel strongly enough to aid me financially.

The local Democrats did what they said they would do. My campaign committee co-chairs, Kevin and Nancy Hill, gave an extremely generous contribution. Eddie and Barbara Atkins, George Mitchell's sister and brother-in-law, gave a major fundraiser, attracting contributions from many local Waterville politicos. Other small fundraisers helped. Finally, we ran one big fundraising event. Bill Hayes and Susan Seaforth Hayes, stars of the television soap opera *Days of Our Lives*, are the parents of Carrie Samuel, a close friend. They donated their time to perform in a benefit for my campaign. Unfortunately the event had to be scheduled over Memorial Day weekend, certainly not the opportune time for an indoor concert. However, because of a major effort by many friends, tickets were sold, dinner parties planned, publicity distributed; and the result was a wonderful evening. The event did not bring a huge profit, but the publicity and good spirits made it an unqualified success.

Money came in to the campaign from many sources. I personally wrote to thank every contributor, whether the gift was large or small. In some cases, even the smallest amount represented a significant sacrifice by the donor. The commitment to my candidacy that such gifts represented affected me in a way I will never forget. In other cases I felt individuals gave less than they could have; however, no one owed me anything, and I was grateful to those people too. Any short-term resentment soon gave way to the realization that I was running for Congress for many of my own reasons. No one else had to see those as being as important as I did.

My goal was to raise $40,000 and contribute $10,000 myself. As primary day approached, I had raised $32,000 and spent $10,000 of my own. With ten days to go, the campaign was all but out of money. I had a large number of volunteers geared to work the district with no literature to distribute. I could not pay for the additional television time to match my opponents'. Budgeting had been fine, but we had not raised the money to meet the budget we planned. No one in the state, not the candidates and not the media, had an accurate picture of what the outcome would be. I decided to exceed my personal budget, allowing my campaign manager to spend another $10,000. I told her to spend what was necessary and not to tell me about it. I knew if I won I would be able to repay myself. And I knew if I lost the money was gone. But I would not be left with doubts about what could have been. More than that, those young people who gave so much of themselves to my campaign would know that I did not back off and let their efforts go for naught. They had to see the fruits of their labors maximized. It was important to me that their idealism was not dampened by my hesitancy. I had serious doubts about our chances of winning the primary, but I also knew that we would all consider the campaign a success if we did all we could right up until the final hours. That was a decision I never regretted.

In retrospect it is clear to me that my campaign was not adequately financed. I could have fruitfully spent another $25,000 to $35,000. That amount would have enabled me to reach more voters with my message, to improve my name recognition, to cut fewer corners. It would not have meant the difference between my defeat and victory. My campaign was directed at a certain type of voter, the issue-oriented, concerned voter. Most of those knew about my campaign, knew where I stood, and supported or opposed me accordingly. An extremely wealthy person could spend a quarter of a million dollars on a campaign in Maine. However, such an expenditure would have resulted in much waste. That amount might be called for in Houston, but it is not necessary to spend that much in order to run a thorough campaign in rural Maine. Even if I had spent that amount, I would still be a college professor today, not a member of Congress.

Some aspects of the way I financed my campaign and the way I feel about fundraising are typical of congressional primaries. However, the variety of experiences is again wide. The way in which the FEC reports its data makes it impossible to determine how much is spent on primary campaigns by those who win primaries and go on to general elections. Thus, the best estimates available on the fundraising experiences in primaries are those from our questionnaire.

A vast majority of those responding, winners as well as losers, felt that their campaigns were not adequately financed. Over three-quarters of those responding (77.9 percent) shared this view. When asked how much more would have been necessary to run the campaign as they wanted, the median response was $33,000. The additional increment that candidates felt they would have needed rose with the amount they actually spent on the campaign, though the range was not great. For those spending under $5,000, the median increment that would have been needed was $25,000; for those spending more than $5,000 but less than $25,000, the increment was $30,000; for those spending more than $25,000 but less than $50,000, $41,000; for those spending over $50,000, $43,500.

It is also interesting to note that many who lost in congressional primaries, with the advantage of hindsight, concluded that they would have lost even if their campaign had been adequately financed. Approximately 20 percent said they would have lost even if they had the money available that they felt would have been sufficient. Another 30 percent said they were unable to say if the additional money would have made a difference in the outcome of their election. On the other hand, the other half of the losers responding did feel that lack of adequate financing was a determinative factor, 20 percent responding that they definitely would have won had they had enough money.

Those whom I interviewed were anxious to talk about the role of money in their campaign. They concentrated on a number of key areas, the difficulty in raising money, the dominance of special-interest money, the advantages that those with money had, and the complexity of solving this problem through public financing. Anyone who runs for office quickly becomes aware of all of these aspects.

The first difficulty encountered was not knowing how to raise money. Political fundraising is a well-honed art form. Novices cannot step in and expect to match those who have been at it for years and years, campaign after campaign. Two losers who ran credible campaigns expressed their feelings:

> If we'd had a couple thousand more dollars, I'd have been happy. But we didn't know how to raise money and it's hard for outsiders in a primary. I said I'd underwrite a mailing. If we got contributions in, then we'd put those into newspapers and radios. They didn't come in.

> We didn't spend too much money because we didn't have the people who knew how to raise it. We did the best of handing out material and getting it all over the city. But we couldn't match the big bucks.

Opinions such as these are common among those who ran in close campaigns and lost. They were serious candidates, impeded because of lack of funds. That is a very different experience from those who never tried to raise money: "I really didn't try to raise money. I didn't have drawings or fundraisers. I just spent a little of my husband's money. It was just that I thought I'd take a shot."

Money did not really play a role in the outcome of that woman's campaign. No aspect of her campaign led one to believe she was serious. She did not have an organization, did not campaign heavily herself, and eventually did not receive many votes. She was, however, on the ballot; she did participate in candidate forums; she confused the voters, as did many fringe candidates.

She was one of those who responded that money had "no importance" in the outcome of her campaign. In that she had little company. Only 8.4 percent of those responding to my questionnaire felt money was of "no importance"; another 20.3 percent felt it of "little importance." The vast majority felt that the role of money was of "considerable importance" (36.7 percent) or that it was a "determining factor" (34.7 percent). These respondents — winners and losers — were commenting not only on their own efforts but also on those of others in the same race.

One of the persistent questions facing candidates is how much of their own money they should invest. This problem was not as serious for the very rich, many of whom determined in advance that they would underwrite their own campaigns, regardless of the cost, nor for the poor, who did not have the resources available to contribute much, as it was for that large group in the middle. Gary Van Brocklin, a young Republican from Youngstown, Ohio, decided to seek his party's nomination but soon backed off: "I wasn't willing to go broke. I talked it over with my wife.

My law practice was just picking up. I would have had to give it up for six months or so. We decided that I couldn't do that. The personal cost was too high.''

Others were in situations similar to my own. They determined that they were willing to make a certain personal sacrifice, of time and of money. As the campaign unfolded, however, it became apparent that that sacrifice was not enough. Many went in deeper than they had anticipated — and lost. That left an unpleasant aftertaste, one that often persisted for some time, at least until the debts were paid off: ''It was a good experience in retrospect, except for the money it cost me. I spent over $20,000 of my own money which I didn't have. I'll be paying that off for years.''

The wide variation among our congressional districts causes another difficulty. Some districts simply are poorer than others; people in those districts cannot afford to support congressional candidates or any other politicians. Mike Synar faced this problem in his successful attempt to unseat Ted Risenhoover: ''We come from a district whose average income is far less than the national average. It's hard to raise money — this isn't a district with a tradition of campaign giving. We did raise some out of this district, but even with a real good effort, it was hard.''

Synar did not say so, but his opponent had less trouble raising money, and Synar himself will have less trouble now that he is in office. Many have commented on the influence of special-interest money in campaigns. Those discussions need not be repeated here. If political action committees (PACs) play a major role in incumbents' success in general elections, they play even more of a role in primaries. On the average, nonincumbent respondents to my questionnaire received less than 5 percent of their money from PACs. Comparable statistics for incumbents are not readily available, but candidates are unanimous in feeling that it is much more. It is sobering to realize that fifty incumbents seeking reelection in 1978 each received more than $70,000 from PACs. As one loser to an incumbent summarized his views: ''PACs tend to be whores. Their first rule is to contribute to incumbents, no matter how they stand on the issues or ideology or anything. Their second rule is to contribute to seeming winners, again regardless of anything. Only after that do they look at the positions candidates take.''

One caveat seems to be in order. PACs also go after their enemies. Congressman Bob Eckhardt (D., Tex, 1967-81) has made a career of angering the oil interests in his district while fighting for environmental causes. A young, articulate trial lawyer named Joe Archer decided to take him on in 1978. Archer knew that Eckhardt had enemies; the challenger would not let his ambition be tempered by any pangs of conscience: ''Had the people downtown known how close this race was going to come out, there is no telling how much I could have raised. . . . I'll take money

Table 4.2 **Cost of Congressional Primaries**

Cost of Campaign* (in Thousands of Dollars)	N	*Percent of Total*	*Winners*	*Losers*	*Number against Incumbent*	*Percentage against Incumbent*
0-5	64	26.4%	10.9%	89.1%	26	55.3%
6-25	57	23.6%	21.1%	78.9%	7	14.9%
26-50	45	18.1%	15.9%	84.1%	4	8.5%
51-100	48	19.8%	29.2%	70.8%	8	17.0%
Over 100	29	12.0%	44.8%	55.2%	2	4.3%
TOTAL	242	99.9%**			47	100.0%

(N = 242)

*See question II.2 on the questionnaire in appendix I for the exact wording of the question and answers.
**Percentages do not total 100 because of rounding.

anywhere I can get it, from any group other than the Nazi party. You have to run against an incumbent.''

The total picture that emerges from a review of the experiences that candidates had in financing their 1978 congressional primaries is not a positive one (see table 4.2).

Half of the candidates spent under $25,000 in their primaries. More than 70 percent of those who ran against incumbents spent that little. All of those running against incumbents and a vast majority of the others who spent under $25,000, lost. These statistics would be even more compelling except that of the thirty respondents in open seats who answered that they spent between $5,000 and $25,000, eleven (36.7 percent) won. If this table were broken down by type of race, that one cell would be the only one in variance from what one would expect if one feels that money is a determining factor in congressional primaries. Even with that exception, these data lead to two clear conclusions. First, challengers to incumbents by and large are not able to raise enough money to mount serious efforts, especially given the power of incumbency. Second, though the fit is not exact, and though anyone running in a congressional primary faces large odds, those spending more money have significantly better chances of winning (cf. Jacobson, 1980).

Because the amount of money raised has an impact not only on the type of campaign run but also on the chances for success, it is important to see the sources from which candidates do raise the money they spend (see table 4.3).

A number of interesting conclusions emerge. First, the more that is spent on a campaign, the lower the percentage of that expenditure that comes from the candidate. In absolute dollars, the candidates who are spending more are also contributing more, but as a percentage of total

Table 4.3 **Sources of Campaign Funds**

COST OF CAMPAIGN* (in Thousands of Dollars)		MEAN PERCENTAGE OF CONTRIBUTIONS FROM:**				
		Small Givers	*Medium Givers*	*Large Givers*		*Fundraising*
Self	*Family*	*(⟨$25)*	*()$25⟨$100)*	*()$100)*	*PACs*	*Events*
0-5	71.1%***	5.0%	5.0%	5.0%	8.0%	3.0%	3.0%
6-25	49.0%	6.0%	11.0%	14.0%	11.0%	4.0%	4.0%
26-50	40.0%	5.0%	13.0%	16.0%	16.0%	5.0%	5.0%
51-100	36.0%	5.0%	10.0%	15.0%	24.0%	6.0%	5.0%
Over 100	27.0%	4.0%	8.0%	19.0%	22.0%	14.0%	5.0%

(N = 243)
*See question II.2 on the questionnaire in appendix I for the exact wording of the question and answers.
**See question II.6 on the questionnaire in appendix I for the exact wording of the question and answers.
***Cell entries are the mean percentage of the total raised in the primary campaign from each identified source.

campaign expenditures the figure descends quickly from the 71 percent from personal funds, spent by those with the least expensive campaigns down to the 27 percent spent in those campaigns costing over $100,000. Thirty-five percent of those spending less than $5,000 answered that they funded their campaigns entirely on their own; only one person who spent over $100,000 did so.

Second, campaigns do not seem to raise very much from candidate's families, nor from small donors, those giving less than $25. Many campaigns expend a great deal of effort in reaching small donors, and certainly there are benefits beyond the financial gains in winning enough commitment to attract any contribution; but small gifts simply do not add up to significant percentages of campaign expenditures. In fact, of the 243 respondents to my questionnaire, only nine (3.7 percent) said they raised more than half of their money in contributions under $25 and all of those were in campaigns with total expenditures of under $50,000. By contrast, 41.5 percent said that they financed more than half of their campaigns themselves, including the 16.1 percent who answered that they financed all of their campaigns personally.

Third, those with the more expensive campaigns receive not only more money but also a higher percentage of their money from big individual donations and from PACs. One difference between the two highest groupings seems to be the ability to raise PAC money. If 14 percent of a $150,000 campaign comes from PACs, that amounts to $21,000, more than is spent on almost half of all of the campaigns. On the other hand, 6 percent of $75,000, typical amounts for the next grouping, is only $4,500, not an inconsequential amount to be sure, but also not a sum likely to be determinative in an election.

Table 4.4 Fundraising Techniques Used in Congressional Primaries

COST OF CAMPAIGN* (in Thousands of Dollars)		ATTEMPTING TO RAISE MONEY BY:**			
	N	Personal Appeals to Friends	Appeals to PACs	Appeals to Individuals Based on Group Membership	Mass Mailings
0-5	98	44.9%	19.4%	18.4%	13.3%
6-25	62	53.9%	43.5%	35.5%	41.9%
26-50	36	83.3%	52.8%	36.1%	61.1%
51-100	31	87.1%	61.3%	58.1%	54.8%
Over 100	22	86.4%	81.8%	50.0%	77.3%

(N = 250)
*See question II.2 on the questionnaire in appendix I for the exact wording of the question and answers.
**See question II.7 on the questionnaire in appendix I for the exact wording of the question and answers; percentages can total more than 100 because multiple responses were possible.

One could argue that the larger campaigns are the only ones that go after PAC money and big givers. Perhaps others would have received more money if they had gone after it. Sophistication in fundraising techniques may lead to more successful efforts and may explain the differences between those who can run expensive campaigns and those who cannot. Table 4.4 attempts to get at this problem. It is difficult to assess sophistication of fundraising efforts. My best approximation identifies the efforts made by various campaigns.

To some extent the data confirm the speculation above. Those who attempt to raise money in more ways are in fact more successful. One notes immediately how few of those spending less than $5,000 even attempted to raise money. I included the question on "personal appeals to friends" to indicate even a minimal effort. Most of those spending under $5,000 did not attempt even that. Again, we see evidence of less than serious campaigns.

However, one should not draw too strong an inference from this table. Those running the more expensive, more sophisticated campaigns do try almost all fundraising efforts. They are more successful in part, at least, because it is perceived that they might be successful. One loser, who tried unsuccessfully to attract PAC money, concluded: "They wanted to know if I was going to win the election. They couldn't care less what I stood for. They simply wanted to buy influence. To be effective you have to have them. The big money is the special-interest money. You can only raise so much in $25 cracks."

Much the same can be concluded about at least one set of major contributors, those large givers who try to become powers behind the throne. Many candidates appeal to these individuals; few are funded. To

Table 4.5 Campaign Debts from Congressional Primaries

COST OF CAMPAIGN* (in Thousands of Dollars)	*Percent Having* *Campaign Debts***
0-5	26.0%
6-25	50.0%
26-50	66.7%
51-100	87.1%
Over 100	95.4%
*Open Seats****	
Winners	53.4%
Losers	55.6%
To Challenge Incumbent in	
Other Party	
Winners	90.0%
Losers	39.7%
Against Incumbent in	
Own Party	41.7%
Total	51.0%

*See question II.2 on the questionnaire in appendix I for the exact wording of the question and answers.
**See question II.10 on the questionnaire in appendix I for the exact wording of the question and answers.
***See note with table 2.1.

a large extent the determining factor is perception of winnability. Serious candidates try whatever type of appeal might be effective. Many are frustrated because appeal after appeal results in little or no success. The result of this frequently is a campaign funded below what the candidate had projected.

Another frequent result is a sizable campaign debt. Fifty-one percent of those responding to my questionnaire answered that they had a debt remaining when their campaign ended. Of those debts, 42.2 percent were under $5,000, another 43 percent were under $25,000. More than half (56.2 percent) of the debts were less than 10 percent of the total campaign budget; however, nearly a quarter of the debts were more than a third of the total amount spent.

Table 4.5 indicates that the more expensive a campaign was, the more likely the candidate was to have a debt remaining at its completion. It also indicates that winners did not fare better than losers in this aspect of campaigning. However, many winners were able to pay off primary campaign debts during the general election, temporary as that solvency might have been.

Candidates tend to wonder how they built up such large campaign debts. They are always amazed that campaigns seem to gather their own momentum, that decisions are made, money spent, and no one asks where the money will come from. Once the campaign is over and the debt remains, no one has to wonder who will pay off the debt: it is the candidate, plain and simple. Approximately a fifth of those with campaign debts said that they would try more fundraising to pay off their debts. Rare indeed is the contributor who will give a substantial amount to aid a campaign that has already lost. Fundraisers may be attempted, but except for winners who develop new resources, most candidates must face their debts alone. The experience is unpleasant and unfortunately is often the one that lasts when the campaign ends.

From this review and the significant literature on campaign financing (see bibliography), we know that serious problems exist in how we fund our congressional elections. Those who have the most money have a tremendous advantage in a primary election. The extent of that advantage varies from district to district, situation to situation, but it is always there. Incumbents have a tremendous advantage in raising money. The 1974 campaign-funding reforms have ''cleaned'' up the process, but they have not had all of their desired effects. FEC regulations do bring openness and accountability; they do remove the influence of the few very large contributors, but they do this at a significant cost.

Part of the cost is the burden borne by those campaigning for office. One of those interviewed pulled out of his campaign early: ''I never really ran. I never raised or spent a cent after the filing fee. But I still had a heck of a time getting rid of the FEC.'' The complexity of the FEC regulations means that many campaigns must hire accountants just to guarantee compliance.[2] However, such burdens are not the worst of the unanticipated consequences of campaign-reform legislation. The worse consequence for congressional elections, evident in primaries to some extent but well documented in general elections, has been the heavy reliance that candidates, particularly incumbents, place on PACs for funding their campaigns.

Why this has happened is simple enough to detect. First, the 1974 reforms make PACs legal. Second, because presidential elections are now publicly financed, totally for the general election and partially for the primaries, more money is available for congressional and other campaigns. The next question to be dealt with is how to counteract this

---

2. The 1979 amendments to the Federal Elections Campaign Act eased the reporting requirements somewhat for campaigns spending under $5,000. Other reporting requirements were also simplified.

unintended and undesired consequence of earlier reforms.

Various proposed reforms have been suggested and introduced in the Congress. One, introduced in the House by Congressmen David Obey (D., Wisc.) and Tom Railsback (R., Ill.), sought to limit the impact of PACs principally by restricting the amount of money a congressional candidate could receive from such organizations. Reforms of this type also seek to increase the amount of money individuals can give to a political campaign.

The other approach has been to extend the concept of public financing to congressional elections. In 1977 a bill calling for public financing of congressional elections was one of the administration's highest priorities. It did not pass. The subject is immensely complex, all the more so if one attempts to apply it to primaries as well as to general elections. Merely listing some of the problems that must be dealt with illustrates this complexity.

The principle of public financing is simple. People should not be able to buy undue influence by contributing to a campaign. This removal of private contributions solves the problem so evident during the Nixon administration. Logic holds that if this is a proper way to finance presidential elections, it should also be proper for congressional elections — and gubernatorial, state assembly and senate, city council, and so on. The logic holds for each level. If private money is to be removed from one level, it will be spent at another, just as more is now spent on congressional elections because presidential elections are publicly funded. Where should it end? Congressman Synar expressed this view: "I think you have to be careful on public financing. I think any bill must be written in a way that is very limited. And it has to be stopped at some level. We can't afford to publicly finance all elections at all levels — local, county, and what not."

One can legitimately ask why we cannot afford to do so. The total "bill" probably would not exceed the biennial advertising budgets of Ford or General Motors. But the fact is that the public and government officials would never permit such an expenditure. The elected officials would fear that the public would see such legislation as benefiting incumbents at the public's expense and would seek revenge at the polls. Their perception might well be accurate.

If one question involves what campaigns should be publicly financed, another involves "who" should be financed in those campaigns. This is particularly troublesome if one is considering public financing for primaries. Problems arise at either end of the spectrum of competitiveness. Of the 870 potential congressional contests for major-party nominations in 1978, 43 attracted no candidates at all; an additional 464 nominations were awarded without contested primaries. One likely consequence of public funding would be fewer seats in which one party did not field a candidate. This is a positive consequence. However, what happens in those 464 cases of uncontested nominations? Should the nominee be funded even though he or she has no opponent? Probably not; but if not, would one not expect phantom candidates to appear to assure that the real candidate received public funds?

At the other end of the competitive spectrum, whom does the government finance in an "eleven-car trainwreck", as one hotly contested primary was classified. Certainly some threshold would be necessary. This step would have a positive effect if it eliminated some of the frivilous candidates. It would have a negative effect if it encouraged them. Moreover, the way to avoid such encouragement would be to set a high threshold. Might this also not discourage some potentially serious candidates who do not have previous experience at raising funds?

Once one has decided whom to fund, one must decide how much money should be given each candidate. The total amount the government will spend is clearly one factor to take into account, but from a theoretical point of view, a more critical factor involves what effect various amounts will have on a particular election. John Porter, a primary winner who lost a 1978 general election in Illinois's Tenth District, concluded: "My only worry about public financing is that it will be used by incumbents to look out for themselves. If you put a limit of say $100,000 — well, that's a lot in some districts, but in this district, it would guarantee that Abner would never lose." Porter won a special election to succeed Abner Mikva after Mikva was appointed to the federal bench. Perhaps his opinion has now changed. However, the point is a valid one. Districts vary so greatly in terms of how much is needed to contest an election effectively that it is very difficult to determine how much public financing is appropriate in order to avoid passing an "incumbent protection" act on the one hand or wasting vast sums on the other.

Because these questions are difficult, even those who should favor public financing of congressional elections have trouble: "I'm against public financing even though I should be for it. I didn't take any special-interest money. But I'm against public financing because it will give incumbents even more safety. I'd favor total elimination of PACs, only allowing individual contributions."

But others could easily point to problems with this solution. Surely it favors the very rich for one thing.

And so it goes. Money is the worst aspect of congressional elections for candidates. The factor that has a determining influence in many campaigns. The factor that clearly evidences the greatest inequities, between incumbents and challengers, between financially well-placed candidates and those less fortunate, between single-issue candidates who can have appeal to PACs and those who are generalists. The factor that is in most need of corrective steps. A factor that stays the same. New reform is unlikely to come quickly. Little will change. And candidate after candidate will continue to echo Hubert Humphrey, attesting that this part of campaigning is "a disgusting, degrading, demeaning experience."

5.
CAMPAIGN
STRATEGY

Those who have run for office were among those most able to empathize with Ted Kennedy when he was so totally unable to articulate why he was seeking the presidency, in that famous interview with Roger Mudd during the fall of 1979. How can one articulate hopes, dreams, desires, aspirations, strengths, and ambitions in a sixty-second answer? In the final analysis, most of us run for office because we want to hold that office, because we feel we can do better in that office than the current occupant, because we care about the direction of governmental policy. These are desires, feelings, beliefs, not hard, cold facts. We are supported most ardently by those who share those desires, feelings, and beliefs and who have faith that we can fulfill them. But the purpose of a campaign is to convince a plurality of the voting public to support a candidate, not necessarily so ardently as to give up time and money and to invest emotional energy in a campaign but at least to the extent of going to the polls and pulling the right lever. To do that a candidate must articulate why he or she is running for office and devise a strategy and tactics for communicating that message.

I *knew* I could serve the people of Maine's First Congressional District better in the Congress than David Emery was serving them. I had worked in the Congress as a staffer; I knew how to get things done. I knew the right people to be effective. I would be a Democrat in a Democratic House. I had thought through what kinds of contributions I, as one junior member, could actually make. I had seen how impotent, legislatively, Emery really was. My friends and supporters shared all of these beliefs.

But I was also a realist. My liberal views on policy were firmly held. My views on controversial issues such as abortion and gun control were uncompromisable. I had to know whether it was possible to run a successful campaign in my district based on the issue positions I felt so strongly about.

I commissioned a poll to answer those questions. Polling is vital to "new-style" politics (Crotty, 1980: 1-28). A campaign with an openended budget should use polling throughout. Polls should not be used just to measure how well one is doing. Polls should be used to ascertain why one is doing as well or as poorly as one is. What parts of the campaign are working? What parts are not? Why are those that are failing, failing? Most campaigns for governor or for the United States Senate use polling for these purposes.

Most congressional primary campaigns cannot afford to use sophisticated polling at all. Only 21.8 percent of those responding to my questionnaire commissioned public opinion polls. Nearly three out of five of those who did not poll did not do so because it was too expensive. Eighty-two percent of those spending over $100,000 in their campaigns polled; none of those used amateurs pollsters. On the other hand, only 13 percent of those spending under $50,000 polled; almost three-quarters of those polls were conducted at least in part by amateurs.

Most congressional primary campaigns that do poll poll only once. A benchmark poll, in other words, a poll to determine one's starting position, is useful in and of itself, but not so useful as in combination with follow-up polls. My poll, like most polls used by congressional primary candidates in 1978, was designed to measure name recognition and to help us develop issues. In asking Bill Hamilton to poll for me, I stated that one purpose of the poll should be to determine if I was a viable candidate. His answer essentially was that I was in the primary but probably would not be against Emery in the fall. I ran anyway. A less biased observer than I might conclude that I was not really interested in learning about my "viability."

Hamilton's poll did stress issues. I knew that few would recognize my name. I did not need to spend the little money I had to prove that. However, I did find out what issues were most important to the Democrats in the district. I found that my views on the economy, on the role of government, on the job of a member of Congress were compatible with those of the voters, if they were stated correctly. I also found out that my pro-choice position on abortion and pro-gun-control position were not anathema to the Democratic voters. Democrats split on these issues; many felt passionately about them, but few said that they would vote solely on these issues. Finally, I found that David Emery was not viewed as incompetent by his constituents, even his Democratic constituents. He was viewed positively, extremely positively, not because of what he stood for or what he had done, but because of who he was, a nice guy, just like us, someone to whom the people could relate. Stressing my competence and Emery's inability to do the job, the themes I intended to develop, would not be effective.

After discussions with my pollster and extended discussions with my campaign manager, I decided on the tack my campaign would take. In the primary I was going to attempt to build up my own image, to attack Emery only on specific points on which he was out of line with the district. I knew that I could never "out common man" Emery. I simply am not "one of the guys." Therefore, I decided that I would build on my strengths, trying to convince the voters that I knew more about the job, the issues, their concerns, than did my primary opponents. I wanted to appear "congressional," not above the people, but the type of representative they would want in Washington. If I got through the primary with that strategy, then I would start worrying about Emery. A lesson seems to have emerged: if no solution to a problem appears possible, postpone dealing with the problem.

To make an impression on someone, you first have to get his or her attention. No one except the few political die-hards cares about a congressional primary six months before it happens. Knowing that the average voter would ignore all of the primaries until election time, I felt it crucial to convince opinion leaders I was a serious candidate whom they should consider. None of the campaigns was visible during the winter of 1978. I decided to take a chance by spending a quarter of my media budget on running a name recognition television spot, at a time when no one was thinking about politics.[1]

The idea was simple. Introduce me to the general public in the hope that they would recall these spots when my advertising started again closer to the primary. But more importantly, let the opinion leaders know I was serious. I was on television four months before the primary.

Because I could only afford one poll, I have no hard evidence of how successful this tactic was. In the commercial and throughout the campaign I wore a wide bow tie. (Even issue-oriented candidates need some gimmicks!) I know I was recognized more on the street after the commercials ran. "You're the guy with the bow tie. Running for something,

---

1. The text of this advertisement appears in appendix II.

aren't you?'' On the other hand, we timed fundraising letters to coincide with the early commercials; they were not noticeably successful. These commercials marked the start of an effort to build an image. From then on I was publicly commenting on congressional issues everyday. I stressed economic issues, the cost of food in Maine, our high unemployment rate, the squeeze felt by those elderly living on fixed incomes. I am confident that I was successful at impressing those who were following the campaign that I had a better command of national issues facing the Congress than did the other candidates. Dick Spencer stressed solving local problems and cutting back the bureaucracy so that it really met citizens' needs. He was quite impressive. Guy Marcotte took the emotionally appealing side of every issue. He had no knowledge of details of problems nor of existing programs, but he could attack Washington, big government, and the Congress with the best of them. He gave his campaign over totally to Ad Media. He was an ideal candidate for them because he would take any position if it seemed electorally beneficial. John Quinn is a thoughtful fellow. He knew little about issues other than consumer affairs. He was uncomfortable speaking without adequate knowledge. Consequently he spoke only on those issues he knew and avoided everything else. He alienated many activists, though probably not many voters, because those following the campaign closely felt he was waffling.

I only had one strategic disagreement with my campaign staff in nine months of working together. That disagreement revolved around the abortion question. Everyone agreed that I should not compromise my views. The question was how strongly I should state them. Most felt I should soft-pedal, not equivocate but not answer attacks either. That was Dick Spencer's strategy. Quinn equivocated, stating that he personally opposed abortion but that he also opposed a constitutional amendment and thus supported the Supreme Court. Marcotte made a direct appeal to the organized anti-abortion groups, implying that those on the other side, frequently indicating Spencer and me, favored killing innocent babies.

I am not passive by nature. I hate demagogues, particularly ignorant, unprincipled demagogues. I agreed with others that Marcotte's tactic was to goad me into an emotional counterattack. But for me the alternatives were counterattack or sit on my hands and quickly develop a severe ulcer. We held a staff meeting and reached no consensus. At the next joint appearance, Marcotte began again. To everyone's surprise, mine included, I interrupted him in the middle of his statement and, quite skillfully I might add despite the immodesty, went up one side of him and down the other, attacking his methods and tactics, never questioning the sincerity of the beliefs of those who shared his views, but pointedly discounting his own sincerity and motives. When I was finished, the audience remained in stunned silence. Marcotte did not respond. The moderator was at a loss. Eventually the moderator recovered and moved to another subject, but the stage was set for future clashes between Marcotte and me. Spencer was relieved that someone was taking Marcotte on, and glad that it was not him. Quinn remained above the battle. Marcotte joined it gleefully, since his strategy was to appeal to those who felt I was a flaming liberal (a label I proudly claim) and our arguments fueled his claims. I felt no regrets either. I doubt that my position helped me electorally, but I know I slept better because of it. In the course of this campaign it became clear to me that a principled position on how one presented oneself was as important as not compromising strongly felt policy views.

The four candidates in Maine's First Congressional District followed four different strategies. Dick Spencer's was the most carefully developed. He based his appeal on solving local problems and developing legislation to do that. He drew on his record in the state legislature and on his ties with local politicians to transmit this message with a personal touch. He was considered a liberal in the legislature but downplayed national issues and his liberal views.

I could not match Spencer's legislative experience, but I drew on my own Washington experience as more relevant. I also talked about the voters' concerns, not local ones but ones that could be addressed through congressional action. I stressed issues, differences between me and the other candidates on issues, and my ability to do the specific job I was seeking.

John Quinn took a totally different track. He never developed an overall strategy. He simply went with what he had, and it worked. I do not believe even today that he knows why he won; if he did, he would have run a different campaign in the fall against David Emery. Again, I feel this is typical of many congressional primaries. Quinn's "strategy" was to rely on high name recognition, from his very visible career as the state's consumer advocate, and to draw on his geographic and ethnic base. He never developed issue positions or appealed to voters on issues beyond the few he knew well. He campaigned heavily among the Irish in Portland and South Portland where he was raised; he effectively used his wife's appeal among the French in Augusta, her hometown. He did extremely well in these areas and few others, but it was enough.

Guy Marcotte was the last to enter the race. He and Ad Media saw an opportunity because the three of us in the race were all perceived, with varying degrees of accuracy, as liberals. Marcotte gave all of his campaign money, mostly borrowed personally, to his advertising firm. Their campaign was highly media-oriented. Without discussing issues, they portrayed Marcotte as a "get-tough, anti-government, anti-liberal fighter

for what's right in America.'' His campaign in many ways was a carica-
ture, but it was nearly effective. York County supported Marcotte loyal-
ly; and this base, combined with those disaffected by government action,
was enough to gain him second place.

These strategies are typical of those adopted in other races across the
country. However, if one wants a catalog of strategies used nationally,
one must be aware of the context of the campaign. Incumbents were
seeking reelection in 382 districts in 1978. Those incumbents were
factors in 253 competitive primaries that were held in those districts. If
the contested primary was not in the incumbent's party, the candidates
seeking nomination had to convince the voters in their party that they had
the best chance to unseat the incumbent in the fall. While pursuing our
own strategies to win the nomination, the four of us running in Maine's
First Congressional District were always aware that the real battle was
against David Emery, not against each other. Of those seeking the
nomination to run against an incumbent, more than 85 percent of my
questionnaire respondents indicated that the incumbent was an issue in
their primary. In more than half of the cases, everyone took on the
incumbent. He or she was essentially the only issue; attacking the
incumbent was the only strategy.

Wynn Norris, who lost a primary to oppose Bob Eckhardt in Texas,
captured this strategic premise: ''Everyone was really running against
Eckhardt. I didn't run against Gearhart. The guy running in the Republican primary who would criticize Eckhardt the most would make the best
show. . . . No one is lukewarm on Eckhardt.''

Eckhardt is, of course, controversial in Texas. However, the strategy
against less flamboyant members, who were often viewed as working
toward cementing their seats in Congress, was the same. Television
anchorman Tom Atkins was recruited by Cincinnati Republicans to run
for their party's nomination. He faced a primary against Stan Aronoff, a
popular legislator in Columbus who was not well known among the
average people on the street. Atkins' campaign theme was that he could
win and Aronoff could not: ''Our whole strategy revolved around our
feeling that Tom Luken would be weakest in this election. We thought
that a well-known person with a record would do well against him. I fit
the bill and the timing was right for me personally.''

Such a strategy is not always successful. In a primary, party loyalists
constitute a good percentage of the voters. Atkins's opponent stressed his
record and experience, claiming that he was popular in his district, that he
had served the party, and that as a party person he would have the best
shot at unseating Luken. Atkins realized that the difference contributed to
his defeat in the general election: ''I appealed to Democrats and Independents as well as Republicans. I don't think Stan had that appeal. But in

a primary, of course, well, you're dealing with family and that really chewed me up.''

If one has a primary contest to gain the nomination to oppose an incumbent, the odds are long. Only 14 of 449 who went this route ended up in the Congress when the Ninety-sixth Congress convened. Candidates in this situation faced two strategic situations, one in the primary and another, perhaps totally different, in November. Some even ignored the incumbent while running in the primary, knowing they would have to change their strategy for the general election. For most, however, the two campaigns' strategies were at least loosely connected.

Those running against incumbents in primaries faced even larger odds. Only 5 of the 166 candidates running in primaries against incumbents in 1978 beat those incumbents. Four of those ended up in Congress; the fifth lost in the general election. My questionnaire responses show that virtually all of those running against incumbents chose to make the member in Congress the main issue. Incumbents' advantages have been well cataloged by commentators of congressional elections (Mayhew, 1974a; Ferejohn, 1977; Fiorina, 1977; Fenno, 1978; Mann and Wolfinger, 1981; and others). The only way incumbents can be beaten, particularly in primaries, is if that key resource, incumbency, can effectively be neutralized or turned against the officeholder. Experience has shown that this is exceedingly difficult.

Mark Cohen ran against Joshua Eilberg in suburban Philadelphia. Cohen was a popular, but not well known, state legislator. Eilberg was a popular congressman whose office was known for excellent constituent service; he was also under investigation for improper use of his office. Eventually, Eilberg was indicted and pleaded guilty to a conflict-of-interest charge. The House Ethics Committee voted to censure Eilberg after the primary but before the general election, which he lost. The significance of this timing was not lost on Cohen: ''If he'd been censured a few months earlier, I'd be the congressman now. He'd done a good job at constituent service. People wanted to give him the benefit of the doubt. There were many people who thought he would be indicted or at least censured earlier. Then they would have supported me.''

Vince Gilmartin entered a large field to oppose Charles Carney in Youngstown, Ohio. Carney had served in Congress for five terms; but he had run poorly in 1976. The steel mills in Youngstown were facing hard times; thousands were being laid off. The city's economy was in doldrums. But Carney's inability to help Youngstown did not make him weak. According to Gilmartin: ''Carney was viewed as vulnerable. That's why there was a big Democratic primary. It wasn't his votes but his antics. He'd made a lot of enemies in the press.'' Carney survived the primary, barely winning by only seventy-six votes. A Republican who sought his party's nomination in the same district observed: "Either Vince [Gilmartin] or Tablack would have beaten Carney one-on-one. Either of them would have won the seat, I think. This is a solidly Democratic district." However, neither Gilmartin nor Tablack, the man who came within seventy-six votes, could run against Carney one-on-one. Carney survived the primary because his opponents split the "anti-Carney" vote. In the general election, Carney had only one opponent, the man who succeeded him in Congress, Lyle Williams.

Those who beat incumbents agree that a challenger must be able to run one-on-one against the officeholder and use his record if the challenger is to have any chance. Congressmen Mike Synar and Martin Frost expressed this opinion in nearly similar assessments of their upset wins. Synar explained: "You can't beat an incumbent unless you can go at him one-on-one. . . . That was one of the biggest things we had to have. I had to keep the field down. . . . We couldn't afford to get lost in an eight-man field." Frost stated: "Had a third candidate been in, he could have beaten me then. . . . I didn't know if there would be a third candidate or not for many, many months. One guy — a black man — filed, and he would have hurt me badly as I got a lot of support from the minorities. But he couldn't win. . . . Eventually the Black community leaders forced him out."

Even when an incumbent is challenged one-on-one, as most are, he wins, unless the incumbent has not been working in a way to protect his job. Corruption led to some of the incumbents' defeats and to close calls for others. In every case where an incumbent had trouble in a primary, the incumbent was the issue. Again Martin Frost's views are instructive.

My opponent blew it off. He never took me seriously. He used television, but he never campaigned. . . . I was able to get support of local elected officials because he was so ineffective. When these people started to surface, people became aware that I was serious. My opponent never became aware, but others did.

The embarrassment factor was very significant. We in Texas have a way of keeping people in Congress for a long period of time. It brings power to the state. You need tremendous inertia to throw an incumbent bent out. But you have to take into account another part of the Texas character — pride. I could get the message across that he was an embarrassment.

One can draw generalizations about campaign strategies beyond the fact that those seeking to unseat incumbents must attack those incumbents. These strategies apply to efforts to gain the nomination against an incumbent and to campaign in open seats.

An obvious strategy is to emphasize one's strengths. Since nearly a quarter of those entering primaries in 1978 had held either state or local office, many emphasized their records of achievement. Candidates played this theme in a number of nonmutually exclusive ways. One subtheme, used by those who had previously represented a large portion of the congressional district while holding another office, claimed that the candidate had already demonstrated electability by the voters, that he or she was well known, and that, therefore, he or she would be the nominee who would serve the party interests best by winning.

Other subthemes stressed prior service. Some candidates, like Dick Spencer, related all they had already done for the voters while serving in the state legislature, the mayor's office, the city council, or wherever. By implication the voter could be assured that the candidate would do even more once elected to Congress. A variation on this theme drew attention to the relevant qualifications for office: "The reason I didn't support him was because he wasn't competent from a legislative viewpoint. He didn't understand the legislative process." Opponents, of course, were not willing to concede their nonqualifications. At two separate points in the same interview, Tom Atkins recapped this aspect, first of his opponent's campaign and then of his own:

> Stan's theme was that the party . . . had endorsed a rank amateur who wasn't qualified to serve in the Congress, not an experienced legislator like himself who had . . . served the people well.

> I tried to show that my experience was the relevant experience. I've been intimately involved with national politicians and national issues. Maybe I'm not a legislative mechanic, but that comes easily. They are all reactors, not initiators.

No candidate feels that he or she is unqualified to serve, but many assume the strategic pose of emphasizing other factors. In low turnout, low saliency, intraparty elections, race, ethnicity, religion, and geography are often crucial variables. The fact that elections often turn on factors having nothing to do with the candidates' qualifications is recognized by those seeking office. Many refer to strategies based around such characteristics in quite explicit terms, at times because the strategies succeeded and at times because these factors hurt their chances. The four examples cited below, a few of many that could have been selected, demonstrate that the voting patterns revealed in my race in Maine, with ethnic and geographic labels changed accordingly, are repeated in many races.

When I first discussed running in Maine, many responded that I had no chance, because I was not a native. In Maine, some added, a native is defined as a fifth-generation resident. I discounted that factor, but in many districts having been born and raised in the district is or can be a factor. Wynn Norris thought it important enough to emphasize his birth-place in his campaign effort: "I'm probably the first native to run from this district in half a century. Eckhardt is from Austin. Gearhart lives in River Oaks, the ritzy section. I live on the trashy side of town. Archer did move into the district, but just to run. I lambasted them all with that. It's really sad. They don't know the people in the district. They don't think we're good enough." Having been born in a district is not a prerequisite if one is to "know the people," but it certainly provides an electoral advantage. Most members of the Ninety-sixth Congress were born in the district they represent.

Many congressional districts are large enough geographically that geographic parochialism plays a major role in candidates' strategies (cf. Key, 1949). Obviously, this is less the case in urban districts that are densely populated and geographically compact than it is in those districts that cover vast expanses. In Maine, I was perceived as a Kennebec County candidate; Marcotte, as a York County candidate; Quinn, as a Portland candidate. None of us rejected the support that came from local ties.

In Pennsylvania, the ballot form encourages voting for local favorites. Dave Robinson, who narrowly lost a Republican primary, explained the voting dynamic: "Saxon eventually killed me. I beat Miller in Allegheny County by a couple hundred votes. I was really going there, but Saxon was the local boy. It was the way they put it on the ballot. Three names said 'Westmoreland County' after them. One said 'Allegheny County.' Then it said, 'Choose One.' Who do you think they'd choose?"

Robert Miller, the winner in the same primary, made a similar assessment, though he went about it from the opposite direction: "Saxon is a very attractive candidate, but he is not at all well known in Westmoreland County. Allegheny County gave him a big part of the vote because he was one of them."

Ethnic appeals are very common in congressional primaries, particularly in races with large fields in districts with significant ethnic voting blocs. Marcotte and Quinn each drew heavily on the support of those with ethnic backgrounds similar to their own. Quinn was very adept at solidifying this support, reminding people of his own "roots" in his television advertisements and having his wife tape radio spots in French for airing on shows popular with Maine's Franco-American voters. Many congressional districts are miniature "melting pots," reflecting the extent to which our country has been populated by immigrants. Large fields of candidates in these districts tend to mirror the ethnic composition of the districts. As examples, look at the large numbers of Irish names on the ballot in Massachusetts's Eleventh Congressional District, the Jewish names in New York's Eighteenth, the Italian and Irish names in Pennsylvania's Twenty-first, in their respective Democratic primaries (see table

Table 5.1   **Democratic Candidates in Selected Districts**

Massachusetts, Eleventh District
Margaret R. Dinnen
Brian J. Donnelly
Sabina Kavanagh
Patrick Henry McCarthy
Patrick F. McDonough
James A. Sheets

New York, Eighteenth District
Carter Burden
Howard S. Katz
Betty G. Lall
Allard Lowenstein
Peter F. Wilson

Pennsylvania, Twenty-first District
Don Bailey
John A. Cicco, Jr.
Edward F. Cooke
June DePietro
Richard C. Grove
Richard A. Halapin
James R. Kelley
Jane J. Manderino
Joseph A. Petrarca
Bernard F. Scherer
Donald C. Thomson

5.1). But ethnic politics is not always predictable. In Pennsylvania's Twenty-first District, fifteen candidates sought to succeed John Dent in Congress. The ethnic composition of the district would lead one to think that Italo-Americans would provide a good electoral base for the right candidate. However, two of the candidates in the Democratic primary felt that ethnic politics worked against their chances. June DePietro had won local office in the Penn Hills section of the district, drawing heavily on Italo-American voters, "but in our primary there were so many Italian names on the ballot that the vote was all split up." John Cicco was never certain that his ethnic heritage was a help, despite the numerical advantage it seemed to give him: "Being an Italian isn't an advantage in this district. We are the largest ethnic bloc by far, but the other blocs together are bigger and the Italians are resented because of the way politics is done around here. Many look for non-Italian candidates.'' John Dent's successor is named Bailey.

Far fewer candidates expressed concern about religious affiliation in determining their strategies than was the case with ethnic background. America has a strong tradition of ethnic pride and loyalty. Religious "pride" is less often an overt factor. Irish or Italian Catholics stress their ethnic heritage, not their religious preference. In districts dominated by one religious sect, such as those in Utah that are dominated by Mormans, politics becomes essentially an intrareligion contest. In most districts, religion, if it is a factor at all, is a hidden factor, talked about by the cognoscenti but not presented openly to the public, as the voters should be above such concerns. John Kennedy's victory in 1960 put the issue to rest.

However, members of small minorities are still concerned about the religious issue. The concern cuts two ways — (1) how much will one's religion hurt at the polls and (2) is it possible to minimize any loss by drawing solid support from co-religionists. I know these factors were important in my own decisionmaking calculus. Others whom I interviewed raised the religion question with me as well. But nowhere was it so significant as in the Tenth District of Illinois, represented in 1978 by Abner Mikva.

The Tenth District had elected Mikva to Congress three times, always by razor-thin margins. He had been beaten once, also in an extremely close race. Mikva is Jewish. The district is heavily Jewish. Many of the Jews are Republicans, liberal on social issues, committed to Israel, but conservative on economic issues, reflecting the affluence of the North Shore suburbs to which many had moved from the South Side of Chicago. Mikva is a liberal. Period. No qualms. Abner Mikva is as liberal as Joe Rauh, a member of Americans for Democratic Action, an ideological, flaming liberal. Yet he won because of his ability to draw voters to him who undoubtedly would oppose some of his ideological views.

Gene Salamon, a self-made millionaire Republican, living in one of the most affluent sections of suburban Evanston, felt he could tap some of Mikva's Jewish strength and produce a Republican victory. His campaign strategy was based on that premise.

Sam Young got only 8 percent of the Jewish vote against Mikva in '76. From a demographic standpoint for him to attract only 8 percent of the Jewish vote meant that, from a political standpoint, there were many people who aren't with Mikva philosophically but vote for him because he is Jewish.

My votes came from those independent people who in the past had voted for Mikva. The Jewish voters here are more Jewish than Democratic.

I'm sure that many people who voted for me in the primary voted for Mikva in November. There tends to be a lot of independent voting among the Jews. This was completely *ad hoc*. We made no open attempt to identify ourself as the Jewish candidate. It had to be subconscious to win.

Salamon lost badly. He ran a sophisticated, visible campaign. In the end, he spent more dollars per vote received than did any other congressional candidate in 1978. But his strategy failed totally. His explanation of his defeat stressed his principal opponent's subtle appeals to anti-Semitism, a concern not foreign to the district that saw the Nazi Party's attempt to demonstrate support for anti-Semitism in heavily Jewish Skokie.

Now they're saying things like Salamon was a JDL candidate or I was a front for Mikva. Can you imagine that? It comes from Porter's camp. . . .

Mikva moved here from Chicago, but about 60 percent of the people in the district have moved up here from there. Yet the other Republicans still call him a carpetbagger.

Porter referred to me as an ''opportunist.'' I think ''opportunist'' and ''carpetbagger'' are codewords for other things. There are real anti-Semitic overtones.

Salamon did not lose because his opponent was anti-Semitic. Salamon, though highly successful in the business world, was a neophyte in the political world. He lost because he did not understand the nature of primary politics. Voters do not always accept a perfectly plausible rationale about why one would be the strongest candidate, particularly if the rationale is left unstated. The voters and particularly the active Republicans knew the other candidates. They had been active; they had served the party and some of the voters in the district before. Salamon did seem to be an ''opportunist,'' one who came out of nowhere and spent hundreds of thousands of dollars, one could say, to ''buy'' a nomination. As John Porter put it: ''Gene Salamon had not been active in politics. When someone told me late in the fall that Gene was going to run, I honestly asked 'What party?' ''

A high percentage of those voting in a primary are party activists. If these people do not know anything about a candidate at all, not even his or her party affiliation, it is unlikely they will support that candidate against known and respected competitors. Gene Salamon devised a strategy, ran a strong campaign, played to his strength. He lost, not because of anti-Semitism, but, in many ways for the same reason that Tom Atkins lost to Stan Aronoff in Cincinnati, because he did not understand the nature of the primary electorate. He never distinguished himself from his opponents in a way that was meaningful to the voters.

Significantly, appeals based on issues have not been mentioned in this review of campaign strategies.[2] Few campaigns in 1978 stressed issues. Those that did tended to be unsuccessful. That is not to say that candidates did not develop issue positions. Rather, candidates developed issue positions to maintain credibility but not to win voters' support. Those candidates I interviewed were nearly unanimous in their feeling that the voters did not care much about the issue content of their campaigns.

Issues aren't important. They mean nothing. I said I wanted to go down and legislate. . . . But that's not what they want in South Philadelphia.

I don't think it can be done on issues. It has to be done with media.

No, there wasn't much discussion of issues. People don't care about that.

No big public issues separated us in the primary. Stan is a plastic man, nuts and bolts type, but he has no imagination. Like Luken, he sees his sole responsibility as handling constituents' problems.

There weren't really any issues which separated us in the primary. Robinson ran a personality campaign. He is an athlete, an Olympic rower. He is probably more liberal than I am, but issues were rarely discussed, so the voters couldn't know that.

I don't know how important issues are, nor do I think they should be. I think Nixon won on issues in 1968. No matter what people say on issues, what good is it if you can't trust them. I really feel people should vote on gut feelings.

These opinions come from primary winners and losers, from liberals and conservatives, from Republicans and Democrats, from veteran politicians and novices. In wide-ranging interviews, most candidates did not mention issues at all. Not one of the winners I interviewed mentioned any policy issue as having had anything to do with his or her victory.

What of the controversial issues that were part of the 1978 political scene? These were evident in my interviews. They played very different roles; none was so prevalent as the noted lack of policy content in most campaigns. In only one of the campaigns that I studied in depth did a candidate run a single-issue campaign. In Nashville, anti-nuclear-power activist Jeannine Honicker ran her campaign based almost entirely on that one policy position. Her campaign was for an open seat, incumbent Clifford Allen having died shortly before the filing deadline. Honicker had intended to run in any case. The local power company proposed to build a large nuclear facility a short distance from her home. Honicker's daughter suffered from cancer; Honicker knew the number of people who

2. This discussion recalls Richard Fenno's (1978) discussion of issues in the districts of members he followed as they interacted with their constitutents.

could be exposed to nuclear radiation and threatened with cancer. She decided to dramatize her issue: "I ran one issue mainly. I didn't come out honest when I talked about the pocketbook issues. Everyone knew health was my issue, the threat to health from nuclear plants. Other issues didn't ring true."

Honicker did not do well at the polls; she felt the city was not geared to respond to issues. But in her own terms the campaign was a success: "It was certainly not a successful campaign in terms of winning votes, but it is the cheapest way in the world to get your issues known. Now the television stations call me whenever anything happens. It has opened a lot of doors to me."

The pro-nuclear side made an impact in the Twenty-first District of Pennsylvania. Westinghouse Nuclear employs 6,000 workers in that district. A group from Westinghouse decided that they would play an active role in the congressional campaign, endorsing a Republican and a Democrat, and helping them through a PAC. Republican winner Robert Miller and loser David Robinson both sought this group's endorsement. Robinson felt somewhat bitter that he was not endorsed:

> There was this group called Concerned Advocates for Rational Energy — CARE. They wanted to take part in the campaign and push candidates who were the best advocates for nuclear power. My opinion is that Miller is part professional. He had gone to campaign school and knew all the issues. I went to these guys and listened and said it sounded OK to me. Miller went in knowing all the details of their issue. They endorsed him and went out and worked hard for him. It might have been a put up job in some way; they were half his campaign workers anyway.

Miller acknowledged their help, though he denied any prior connection: "The issue didn't divide us, but it made me a spokesperson for nuclear energy. . . . They endorsed me. . . . It helped a great deal. Their constituency controlled a large bloc of votes."

I found no evidence that Miller's endorsement was a preordained conclusion. Like Salamon, Robinson was naive about the realities of congressional politics. If a candidate expects the endorsement of a single-issue group, he cannot appear neutral and uninformed. Miller was not a professional; he was a well-informed candidate with a specific goal in mind, endorsement by a special-interest group. Robinson was a rank amateur. The CARE PAC endorsed the candidate who best served its interests.

While the pro- and anti-nuclear groups campaigned on a fairly high level, the same cannot be said of the so-called Right-to-Lifers, the activist anti-abortion group. No candidates I interviewed were involved in campaigns with single-issue Right-to-Life candidates. A number, however, faced the active and vehement opposition of anti-abortionists. One primary loser felt this policy issue was critical in his campaign:

> I thought everyone came out the same on issues. It was a tough campaign to make issues important because everything everyone was talking about was the same and we were all advocating the same views. . . . But Pro-Life was the turning point. I said I went along with the Supreme Court and that I knew my opponents were strong politically but they would just have to be against me. One of my opponents picked that up and labeled me the pro-choice candidate. He went the rest of the way with the Pro-Life group.

Another candidate, this one a primary winner, had a more painful experience. While none of the candidates had the support of those opposing abortion, this one candidate was singled out as the enemy by those active on this issue. She and her family were verbally attacked throughout the campaign. Dead fetuses were left on her doorstep. She felt there was no evidence that their attacks made a difference in the margin by which she won or in her general election defeat, but their methods soured her on politics: ''The irony is that they have no regard for people's lives at all. I wouldn't back down to them, but it isn't worth it. They're successful, if they are, because those on the other side are too decent to stoop to their level. Someone has to fight them, but it'll be someone else next time.''

Other candidates had similar experiences. The anti-abortionist, while not very successful in House elections in 1978, made an impact on the individuals who were running, in some cases a lasting impact: ''I don't know about 1980. We think 1980 looks very tough in Indiana. The Right-to-Lifers tasted success in Iowa and they're going to come out in droves to beat Birch Bayh.''

The final issue that was in some evidence was the anti-government, anti-welfare appeal. A number of candidates reflected the views of the frustrated, angry, white middle class. Playing to the emotions that these people feel posed no problem. However, some candidates went so far in expressing these views that they fell prey to what might be called ''indignation overkill'': ''I'm pretty controversial and get some bad press. But just because I only want welfare for those who can't work, because I want to get the cheats off welfare, that doesn't mean I'm racist. What about the civil rights of us poor working slobs who pay for everything? Why do only blacks have civil rights?'' Political journalists felt that 1978 would be a good year for the anti-government candidates to take advantage of those sharing the Archie Bunker mentality. A number of campaigns adopted this strategy, but the candidates espousing those views are not in Congress today.[3]

Over half of the candidates entering congressional primaries in 1978 had never run for office before. Few have the instincts to jump right into a major campaign with an effective strategy. Skip Lange had thought about running for Congress for some time, but 1978 was the first year in which he committed himself to a full-fledged effort: "I had no idea what the role of a candidate was when I started out. What was I supposed to do? What was I supposed to say?"

Like much else that goes on in a congressional primary, candidates develop strategies by trial and error. What appeals seem to work? What feels good as it is being expressed? Some candidates stumble upon strategies that are extremely successful. Some never develop strategies, but win despite themselves. Others tie themselves to well thought-out strategies that are doomed to failure.

Campaigning for office is both art and science. In some races all of the variables are well known to all of the participants. Campaigns turn into "nuts and bolts" exercises. The winner is merely the best mechanic, the most skilled practitioner. Few primaries, particularly congressional primaries, fall into this group. Strategically those campaigns are of two types. Many are foregone conclusions. Incumbents generally are not beaten; most win by large margins. In races not involving incumbents, often one candidate starts with an insurmountable lead, because of name recognition, money, whatever. Other candidates flounder, unsuccessfully, to find the key to break the frontrunner's stranglehold on the nomination. Many of these campaigns never get off of the ground.

In the hotly contested primaries, strategic considerations are often crucial. In setting strategy, the requisite skills are those of an artist, not a scientist. Candidates and campaign managers must get a feel for the district, for the voters, for their concerns; and they must devise a strategy to demonstrate that the candidate relates to each of these. No magic formula exists. Districts differ; candidates' situations differ. What is successful in one congressional primary might be totally inappropriate in a primary in the neighboring state or even in the same district in another year. Many candidates have failed by copying carefully a strategy that worked marvelously in another place at another time.

Strategic planning for congressional primaries is especially difficult because of uncertainty about the most critical variable of all, who will

---

3. In 1980, with President Reagan leading the battle, many who felt that the government should be doing less were elected. By 1980, however, a new economic theory was the basis for many candidates' campaign rhetoric.

vote. One characteristic seems common throughout the nation; voters do not care very much about these races.

In Ohio: I lost because the turnout was low. The turnout was low because people don't care about primary elections.

In Pennsylvania: There's a great deal of apathy here. It's hard to get people to go out to vote. They complain, but they don't vote.

In Texas: For established politicians the apathy was particularly upsetting. They thought they were important.

In Illinois: We have a very low turnout in primaries. It might be because of our system — you have to go in and ask for a party's ballot — but I think it is just apathy.

In California: I don't think people care enough about primaries. It is the most important election for the voters, but they don't recognize it as such. Nationwide the emphasis can't be put on the primaries like it should.

If voters do not care much about an election, the key is to find some appeal that will get voters out to support one candidate for a particular reason. If an incumbent is running or if one candidate is better known than the others, particularly among regular primary voters, those most concerned with politics, then that candidate's strategy is simple. Don't rock the boat. Let inertia carry the day.

For others the task is much more difficult. Unless a specific issue is pressing — either in the nation, as was the case with the Vietnam War in the late 1960s, or in the particular district, as might be the case if a major industry is threatened because of government action or inaction — candidates have not been successful in campaigning based on policy appeals. The average voter does not care enough about most issues to be motivated to become involved in politics. Candidates have to get the feel for the salience of issues; those who understand what the voters are thinking have a chance at winning; those who do not, lose.

Policy issues do not play a central role in most congressional primaries. Other strategies emerge — attack an opponent, appeal to ethnic groups, ally with others seeking more visible offices. Candidates grope. Some succeed, but most fail. If the correct answers were easily discerned, then the peculiar nature of congressional primaries would change radically. But the answers are often obscure, only the successful artist sees them and can paint them into a winning strategy. That's why they call it politics.

6.
CAMPAIGN
TACTICS

Nowhere does the sports analogy fail more completely than in the analysis of tactics used during a political campaign. Before the Dallas Cowboys take the field, Tom Landry and his coaching staff have developed thick offensive and defensive playbooks; they have computerized their opponent's "tendencies" in certain situations; they have worked on contingency plans involving trick offensive plays or special defenses; and they have drilled their team endlessly until game situation actions become almost instinctive. Before the average primary campaign starts for those seeking a seat in Washington's political "stadium," a candidate and his or her close associates might plan a basic tactical approach to implement a rather sketchy strategy; they might draw up a tentative budget, based on inaccurate income and cost projections; they might decide what they want to have done in the field by the candidate and the workers, though the number and ability of those workers is totally unknown. Frequently they cannot think about their opponents because they do not even know who those opponents will be. They cannot set contingency plans because they cannot foresee most situations that might arise. As one candidate put it, a congressional primary tends to be one long "ad hoc" experience.

Three aspects of campaign tactics should be discussed separately.

First, what does the candidate do with his or her time? How does that relate to the activities of campaign workers? How are the human resources of the campaign used? Second, how are the financial resources of the campaign used? How was the money for the campaign spent? How much went to paid media? Of what types? How much went to literature, posters, buttons, bumper stickers, and the other paraphernalia familiar to casual observers of politics? What other devises did the campaign use to get its message across? Third, how did the campaign relate to the news media covering politics in the district? In many districts that question should be reversed. How did the news media relate to the campaign? Campaigns make an impact on the electorate through personal contact, through various forms of advertising who a candidate is and why the candidate should be elected, and through coverage in the local media. Candidates must make a number of tactical decisions in order to maximize the amount of "free" media coverage they obtain. If all is left to chance, in most areas the media will ignore primary candidates. However, in many areas the media's role is central to determining the outcome of an election.

CAMPAIGNING BY THE CANDIDATE

As one who has worked on many primary and general election campaigns for all sorts of offices, I thought I knew a good deal about what a candidate for office did. I was wrong. Nothing amazed me more than how different a campaign looked from the perspective of a candidate from how it had looked as a campaign manager or worker. This was a revelation shared by many of those I interviewed. Once the decision to run has been made, what does one do with oneself upon arising each morning? I referred to my ex-mother-in-law earlier, because her inquisitiveness about how I spent my time was shared by many friends who were close to me, but on the periphery of my campaign.

I made two decisions very early in my campaign that shaped many that were to follow. First, I vowed that I would sleep at home as many nights as was physically possible. I decided this because I did not want to be apart from my children more than was absolutely necessary. I did not feel that that would be fair to them; in addition the decision reflected my view of the office I sought. I have known too many members of Congress who have left their families behind, often literally but, more important, also emotionally, when they entered the House. My priorities were different from theirs. I do not feel that service in Congress should preclude a normal life. To the contrary, I feel one can serve better if one remembers the pressures and concerns of family and friends, if one can avoid being caught in the web of power that envelops the Capitol. Gordon Weil suggested that I campaign actively on that theme, that my concern would be refreshing, different, and perhaps electorally appealing. I never pursued that tack as actively as he would have liked. However, I did maintain my commitment to my family throughout the campaign. Not sleeping out on the campaign trail was a symbol of this commitment; it gave my scheduler a good deal of difficulty and cost me and my staff hundreds of hours of sleep. However, the decision was one I never regretted. My children were a part of my campaign in a way that was fun for them; they were never exploited. And I stayed part of their normal lives while I was running. I may have missed some opportunities to meet voters while attending first-grade plays and birthday parties, but my children came away from the experience feeling that they had been part of something very important to me, not resenting that awful campaign that took Daddy away.

The second important decision was that I would continue to work full-time while running in the primary. This decision had both practical and philosophical roots. The practical aspect of this decision was economic. I could afford a certain amount of time without a salary, but not a full year. Therefore, I decided I would campaign in the primary around my teaching schedule. If I won the primary, I intended to take a leave of absence for the general-election campaign. (In my subconscious, I also knew that if I lost the primary, I would use my pending sabbatical to recover!) I also felt it important to maintain my Colby ties in order to recruit as many student volunteers as possible. I wanted my students to remember that I was really one of them as they were campaigning for me. If they saw me on the campus and in the classroom, I hoped they would be stimulated to work harder. On the other hand, by remaining in the classroom and in contact with my colleagues, I could also monitor my volunteers' academic work to be certain none was getting into trouble on my account.

I arranged my teaching schedule to allow for a maximum amount of campaign time. In truth, I was a lousy teacher during the spring semester of 1978. My students, even those not involved in my campaign, learned a lot about politics. But my heart was never in the classroom; I probably alienated more students because I was not doing the job they had come to expect than I stimulated by my distracted presence. Few of my students remember fondly the lectures I wrote during the one-hundred-mile car ride returning from an early morning factory shift change in Kittery in time for a 9:30 A.M. class. My campaign schedule was full only during vacations and after classes ended in May. This part-time status certainly harmed my own effectiveness.

Many running in 1978 shared my problem about how much time one could give to a campaign. The average candidate campaigned actively for about six months before a congressional primary. Of those responding to my questionnaire, 38.5 percent held no outside job while campaigning;

the same number, 38.5 percent, maintained full-time employment while running for Congress, though many of these were public officials who were not so diligent in fulfilling their duties as they might have been had they not been campaigning. The remaining 23 percent held part-time jobs during their campaigns.

Candidates were also asked how many hours a week they spent campaigning. For those who continued in another job during the primary, the median amount of campaign time during the month preceding the primary was thirty-five hours a week; during the five months before that, it was nineteen hours a week. Full-time candidates could and did spend more time. As one primary winner put it: "I was out stumping all day, every day right from the start. . . . I believe everything counts so it had to have carry-over effects." The data reported on time spent campaigning reflect this commitment. The median number of hours per week spent by full-time candidates during the month preceding the primary was seventy-one; during the five months prior to that, it was fifty-one.

When one looks further into these data, some interesting differences appear. First, those who ran the more expensive campaigns were more likely to campaign full-time; 48.3 percent of those spending over $25,000 campaigned full-time, while only 33.2 percent of those whose campaigns cost less than that amount did not have outside employment. While not many women ran in these primaries (only about 10 percent), over half of those who did campaigned full-time, as compared to 37 percent of the male candidates. However, little difference existed between winners and losers; 40.8 percent of the winners campaigned full-time, and 37.5 percent of the losers did so.

How much time one spends campaigning should be less important than what one does with that time. What contact does the candidate have with the voters? With what voters? How does this relate to what staff members and volunteers are doing? My most general instruction to my scheduler was to fill my days, to black in my class time and fill every other hour.

However, my more specific instructions related to a story Robert A. G. Monks told to one of my classes. Monks is a wealthy Republican who challenged Senator Margaret Chase Smith in the Republican primary in 1972. That race drew national press attention. Over Memorial Day weekend, two weeks before the primary, a *New York Times* reporter was following Monks as he campaigned. To contrast his vitality with Senator Smith's aged appearance, Monks spent Memorial Day walking around Sebago Lake, greeting those enjoying the opening of Maine's summer vacation season. He felt he had a marvelous day, personally greeting 514 citizens, discussing his campaign. In an end-of-the-day interview, however, the reporter deflated much of Monks' enthusiasm, informing the candidate that of the 514 hands he had shaken, only 27 belonged to

Chart 6.1 **Typical Full Campaign Day Schedule**

6:00 A.M.	Leave Clinton, pick up driver, go to Augusta
6:45 A.M.	Greet workers at Statler Paper, Augusta
8:00 A.M.	Breakfast meeting with Augusta organizer and possible workers
9:00 A.M.	Tour of Central Maine Power, Augusta
11:30 A.M.	Shake hands at morning bowling league
12:30 P.M.	Lunch with potential contributor
2:30 P.M.	Shift change at Lipman Poultry, Augusta, followed by meeting with Lipman family
3:30 P.M.	Drive to Portland
4:30 P.M.	Shake hands at Portland Shopping Center
6:00 P.M.	Door-to-door with local organizer in Portland
8:00 P.M.	Candidates' Night in Cape Elizabeth
10:00 P.M.	Drive back to Waterville
11:30 P.M.	Greet night shift at Keyes Fibre, Waterville
12:15 A.M.	Brief meeting at Waterville headquarters
1:00 A.M.	Home to bed

individuals who were citizens of Maine enrolled as Republicans. To paraphrase Barry Goldwater, Monks had not gone "where the ducks were." I wanted to spend my time with voters, Democratic voters likely to cast a ballot in the primary. The problem, of course, was in knowing how to find those voters.

I am not certain that such a thing exists as a typical day during a primary. However, the schedule that appears in chart 6.1 would not be atypical for a full day of campaigning.

Some details deserve highlighting. Days started early and ended late, for me and for my campaigners. I always had a driver with me. This served three purposes. First, by the middle of the campaign, I was always too tired to drive, certainly at night. Some of my "drive time" doubled as "sleep time." Second, it gave student volunteers a chance to be with me, to have more of the feel of the campaign because of proximity to the candidate. Third, I had a chance to do the kind of campaign work — and schoolwork — that could be done in the car. I learned to read in a moving car during this campaign. I read, edited, and rewrote more issue papers on I-95 between Brunswick and Augusta than I would have thought possible. I personally thanked every campaign contributor; most of the notes were written while the car was moving (and the handwriting, if not the thought, reflected that). When I fell behind in any aspect of the campaign or in my teaching preparation, I asked to be scheduled for a couple of hours in the office. I resented losing that time and avoided it whenever possible.

While the schedule appears to be incredibly full, some flexibility is built into it. Two stops — the morning bowling league and the afternoon shopping center — were essentially fillers. If I had time between stops with relatively fixed starting points, my scheduler found a place where people would be and sent me on my way. Some stops, particularly factory shift changes, had to be hit at specific times and were of predictable duration. Workers come in within twenty minutes of when their shift starts. They are receptive to a greeting and will accept campaign literature, though a large proportion of the literature handed out ends up on the floor inside the factor gate. We learned two lessons. First, we handed them an item they wanted, not just a brochure. We gave out wallet-sized Boston Red Sox schedules with my name and picture on them; these lasted throughout the summer, far longer than my candidacy. Second, we always cleaned up after we visited a gate. Again, a number of purposes were served; management was not angry; we "recycled" some material; and I did not face the ultimate degradation of seeing people walking all over my face. Workers leaving a shift left within three minutes of the shift's end; greeting was impossible and, in fact, resented. Handing out schedules was the best we could accomplish.

Other stops were set for specific times but were of unpredictable duration. Lunch with a potential contributor could last from an hour to three, with no necessary correlation between the length of the meal and the size of the check. One of my least fond memories is of a two-hour lunch with a very wealthy supporter. At the end of the meal he handed me the check for the meal and a check for my campaign; they were approximately equal, leading to my personal opposition to "three-martini" lunches.

Some stops were distasteful. Candidates differ greatly on how they approach door-to-door campaigning. Two of the primary candidates I interviewed provided these contrasting assessments:

> It all comes down to one person going out and ringing doorbells and asking for people's votes. That's the way I love to campaign.

> You have to be brash to go into people's homes and ask them to vote for you when you can't even really tell them what you're going to do if you are elected.

My feeling falls somewhere between those extremes. I had no trouble asking people to support me, and I could tell them why I needed their support, but I did feel I was imposing when I asked myself into their living rooms. However, during a campaign a candidate is often at the mercy of local volunteers. On the typical day presented, I had to go door-to-door when it was convenient for my local worker; she was well known in her area and knew the people well. I felt that 6:00 to 7:30 in the evening was an inappropriate time. She felt her neighbors would be home and would be impressed by a stop-in. Two days in advance she canvassed the neighborhood, saying I was coming. I had no choice. Often one feels "up" or "down" after a campaign appearance. I never had a definite feeling as to whether this stop was a success or a failure.

Finally, some stops were obligatory but were probably wastes of time. Candidates' nights fell into that category. I went to each one, often going hours out of my way, often rearranging an entire day's schedule around one candidates' night. I went because I knew the others would be there. They went because they knew I would be there. Usually two or three campaign workers were with me, a driver, maybe another student, a local organizer. Spencer, Quinn, and Marcotte arrived with three or four supporters too. Generally we spoke to the most active politicos in the area. Their minds were well made up. We gave our set speeches over and over. Boring beyond belief.

Two of the candidates in the Twenty-first District of Pennsylvania were among the many I interviewed who shared my feeling that joint appearances were not the educational experiences for the electorate that one hoped they would be:

There were a bunch of candidates' nights or meetings, two a week. What a waste of time.

Eleven candidates. You've heard them a thousand times and they've heard you. The only people in the audience are their supporters and yours. You maybe sway three or four votes in a night. If you win by two, it's a landslide.

Even more callously another in that same race commented: "It became a traveling road show. We all knew each other's speeches. Once we went to an old folks home for a candidates' luncheon. All eleven of us. There were seventy-five people there for lunch; I remember thinking it was a great turnout. When the chairman said it was time to hear from the candidates, all but four or five got up and left. And they were too old to leave without help."

Before I interviewed other candidates, I thought I was the only one so discouraged by these events. But it was a universal phenomenon, a seemingly good way to reach voters that just did not work. The only candidates' night I truly enjoyed was a very poorly attended event sponsored by the Rotary Club in Bath. Quinn and Marcotte, in their wisdom, chose not to attend. I knew that most Rotarians are Republicans; there were only a few potential voters in the room. When I was called on first, I decided to have some fun. I thanked the chair, greeted the Rotarians and Dick Spencer and his campaign aides, and proceeded to give Spencer's speech. I thought the student driving me was going to die laughing. Spencer rose in his turn, made a funny comment about my

Table 6.1 **Candidates' Campaign Activities**

Activity Undertaken*	Nearly Every Day	Many Times a Week	About Once a Week	Sometimes	Almost Never	Never
Visiting factories and/or gates	4.4%**	9.6%	15.2%	19.6%	10.4%	41.2%
Visiting shopping areas	11.2%	23.9%	18.7%	22.3%	6.4%	17.5%
Door-to-door campaigning	18.3%	20.7%	10.0%	17.9%	9.2%	23.9%
Working in office on organization	27.1%	21.1%	16.7%	10.8%	6.8%	17.5%
Working in office on issues	22.4%	26.8%	18.0%	13.6%	3.6%	15.6%
Meeting key people	21.5%	29.5%	18.7%	11.6%	6.4%	12.4%
Delivering speeches, etc.	23.5%	38.2%	17.9%	11.2%	1.6%	7.6%
Attending coffees, parties	13.2%	23.6%	16.0%	18.4%	7.2%	21.6%
Participating in political party functions	6.4%	25.9%	26.3%	23.5%	6.4%	11.6%
Traveling	45.0%	15.1%	8.4%	7.6%	4.8%	19.1%

(N = 251)

*See question III.12 on the questionnaire in appendix I for the exact wording of the question and answers.

**Cell entries are percentage answering each frequency for each activity. Row totals do not always total 100 because of rounding.

increasing wisdom, a comment that no one else understood, and went on to give the same speech, with only slight variations. No one in the audience noticed, but it turned an otherwise full evening into an amusing event for those of us touring the district together. The only problem was the nagging question plaguing both Spencer and me: what had Quinn and Marcotte found to do that was better than this? Quinn had spent the evening with his family; Marcotte had played a twilight nine holes of golf. We had indeed been one-upped.

One final comment on this typical schedule involves travel. I could have spent the night in Portland and done two Portland factories. I chose not to do so. This day was typical in that I drove or was driven about 200 miles, four to five hours in a car. Some of the time was productive, but most of the 25,000 miles I traveled in those six months were painful miles. I still saw little of my children; they were rarely up between 1:00 A.M. and 6:00 A.M., so I had to make other accommodations for time with them. Six months of this type of effort is hard work. I learned a great deal, not the least of that was the extent of my physical stamina.

A candidate's day should also be examined because of what it says about how workers on a campaign must spend their time. Obviously the entire day requires planning, and that takes staff time. In addition, some campaign stops require advance work to be effective. I feel this is especially true of door-to-door campaigning. Other stops cannot be effective without workers supporting the candidate's effort. If a candidate intends to greet workers arriving for the morning shift at a plant at which 300 workers punch in at 7:00 A.M., that candidate will make no visible impact unless volunteers are there helping to hand out literature and with signs telling all who pass by who the candidate is. This help comes best from a worker at the plant but often must be supplemented by other volunteers. If volunteers are with the candidate, they cannot be somewhere else in the district at the same time. Campaign managers must take this into account when planning how best to use their organizational resources.

Table 6.1 lists ten activities that candidates often engage in during political campaigns and shows responses to my questionnaire indicating how frequently each activity was done. One of the most noteworthy aspects of this table is the clear difference in campaign activities. For example, 35.2 percent of the sample visited shopping centers many times a week; 23.9 percent almost never visited shopping centers. Work in the campaign organization was engaged in many times a week by 48.2 percent, daily by 27.1 percent; 17.5 percent never worked in the office an hour while their campaign was functioning.

Cumulative differences can be seen as well. If one looks at individual responses to this question, it appears that some candidates engaged in all or at least most of these activities with some frequency, checking one of the top three categories. On the other hand, the frivolous candidate appears most evident once again. Many respondents answered "almost never" or "never" for each activity. Those candidates undoubtedly ran campaigns similar to June DePietro's in Pittsburgh: "I didn't campaign that much. . . . Lots of people didn't know I was running until they saw my name on the ballot." She really was not running, and she did not receive many votes. But in many districts, particularly in large fields, the few votes garnered by these marginal candidates were determinative.

As a defeated candidate, I have a great deal of sympathy for George Tablack, a leader of the Ohio legislature who gave up a great deal of power and a safe seat to challenge Charles Carney in Youngstown: "I didn't want to run for Congress. I was one of the top Democrats in the House, one of the top five. But the big guys were sitting on their hands. I said, 'I've got to do it. Someone does.' I had to do it for the Valley and for the party." The motivation of one of the others in Tablack's race was quite different: "I had a brother killed in the War at nineteen. That's what this country is about. The boys in Arlington. They died so that people like you and I could run for Congress. I did it for him." "The big guys" eventually got off their hands. The Democratic primary was hard-fought. If Tablack had won the primary, he probably would have been elected in November. He would have been the strongest general-election candidate. But he lost the primary by seventy-six votes, 0.2 percent. Carney survived this primary challenge but lost the general election to a Republican who had an easy primary. Tablack feels he lost not because of "the big

Table 6.2 **Comparison of Democratic and Republican Candidates on Selected Activities**

ACTIVITIES UNDERTAKEN*	DEMOCRATS (N = 137)		REPUBLICANS (N = 114)	
	Daily or Many Times a Week	*Never or Almost Never*	*Daily or Many Times a Week*	*Never or Almost Never*
Visiting factories and/or gates	21.3%	42.7%	5.2%	62.3%
Meeting key people	48.2%	20.5%	55.7%	16.6%
Attending coffees, parties	31.4%	29.9%	53.4%	26.4%
Participation in political party functions	27.7%	24.1%	37.7%	10.5%

*See question III.12 on the questionnaire in appendix I for the exact wording of the question and answers.

guys,'' but because of the 4 percent drawn off by the candidate who ran for ''the boys in Arlington,'' who essentially did not campaign at all. He is bitter, openly wondering whether a fringe candidate cost him a seat in Congress. His experience is the most extreme I came upon but not different in type from many other primaries where fringe candidates held the balance between those running more serious campaigns.

Not only were there differences between those campaigns that were most serious and those that were decidedly less so, but significant differences were also in evidence between Democrats and Republicans, between those running expensive campaigns and those running more modest campaigns, and among those running in different parts of the country. Some of these merit exploration (see table 6.2).

Primary candidates tend to go where their voters are. Democrats and Republicans, at least as candidates perceive them, do not work in the same places, do not live in the same places, do not respond to candidates in the same way. The most notable difference is that many more Democrats greet workers at factory gates than do Republicans. While this difference is substantial, one would think that it might be even more so. A large majority of blue-collar factory workers are Democrats; one would expect nearly all Democratic candidates to seek their votes. Those who do not are either the least active candidates or those who run in districts with few factories. On the other hand, relatively few factory workers are Republicans; those Republicans frequently greeting workers at gates might well be those who were looking past the primary and ahead to the general election. However, the data do not reveal the motivation for engaging in or refraining from specific activities.

Republicans attended informal campaign gatherings — coffees, parties — far more frequently than did Democrats. One logical explanation revolves around the life-styles of most Democrats and Republicans. Apparently, more Republican candidates felt that their copartisans would be comfortable meeting candidates and listening to their appeals in this setting than did Democrats. Had the questionnaire asked about union meetings or VFW halls, the opposite pattern might well have been observed.

The differences observed in attendance at party functions and in meeting key people, while not so substantial, are also worthy of note. Normally, when we think of strong party organizations, we think of the big-city Democratic machines. Political observers (for example, Crotty and Jacobson, 1980) have been noting the passing of such machines for some time. Their disappearance seemingly has left a void in the Democratic party. Democratic candidates attend party functions less frequently than do Republicans. In those districts that I explored in depth, the party provided a forum for Democratic candidates; but party support was not critical to success in the primary, except where the skeletons of machines were still in evidence.

Republican organizations played a different role. Most of the Republicans I interviewed said that the ''organization'' as such did not exist. Rather, there were key individuals who spoke for the Republican party. These individuals were capable of providing or withholding support, particularly financial support, for perspective candidates. Those seeking office had to contact these power brokers, thus a likely explanation for the fact that Republican candidates spent more of their time in this kind of activity.

Another interesting, and perhaps related, difference noted is that those who ran more expensive campaigns spent more time with key people. It has already been noted that candidates themselves are best at raising money for their campaigns. Most individuals who are going to give $500 or $1,000 to a campaign would like to meet with the candidate him-or herself. Surrogates will not suffice. Those who run expensive campaigns, except those who finance the campaigns themselves, must attract big contributors. This necessitates personal contact. Of those who spent over $50,000 in their campaigns, 41.5 percent responded that they spent some part of nearly every day meeting with key individuals; another 39.6 percent said they did so many times a week. On the other hand, of those spending under $25,000, only 12.5 percent met with key people daily, only 27.5 percent did so many times a week.

Contributors surely are not the only ones who must be met with individually. However, early in a campaign, particularly, these meetings are a good use of a candidate's time. How a candidate uses time and how he or she deals with these people again reflect the differences in campaigns.

Anthony Hall lost to Mickey Leland for the Democratic nomination to succeed Barbara Jordan in Houston. Leland and Hall did not enter the race at the same time. In retrospect, Hall felt that Leland gained an all but insurmountable advantage from his headstart:

There were two considerations. First, he ran for a long time. Barbara [Jordan] was perceived as and was unbeatable. I wouldn't have thought of running against her. When Carter was inaugurated, there was lots of talk of Barbara going into the Cabinet. Well, Mickey started running then, making the rounds, you know, and he never stopped. I didn't do it because I didn't want to get Barbara mad or antagonize her people, but it really helped him.

Second, Mickey raised a lot of Jewish money by going out early and seeing those people and making the commitments they wanted. I think half of his money was Jewish money, and he could outspend us because he went out early and got them. He got a lot of people tied up early and it's a closed circle.

Joe Archer's primary against Bob Eckhardt was in another of Houston's congressional districts. Archer knew he would need a lot of money. He, too, started early, seeing key people. However, rather than tying up one group and garnering their support, Archer took an eclectic approach. His campaign was based not on his own appeal but rather on drawing together all of those who had anything against Eckhardt. This tactic in approaching people caused Archer some anguish, though his ambition helped him to overcome any qualms he might have had: "I think the most degrading thing was the necessity to be all things to all people. You can't be truthful. You don't lie, but it's how you pitch it to different people. I didn't start out like that. I didn't want to do it, but I soon learned you had to if you wanted to get anywhere. I felt I was compelled to be somewhat dishonest, not by commission but by omission."

How candidates spent their time is one of the few variables that show regional differences. Too often observers forget the diversity of our country when commenting on congressional elections. However, from these data it is evident that candidates in different parts of the country spend their time in different ways, ways that perhaps reflect different life-styles (see table 6.3).

The differences are not consistent across the regions. However, the data seem to reveal that candidates in the Northeast and Midatlantic states engage in less personal campaigning than do those in other regions, particularly the Midwest,[1] Mountain, and Pacific states. Candidates in the Northeast and Midatlantic states meet voters where they work or where they shop; in the other regions factories and shopping centers are

1. The only state seriously underrepresented by my respondents was Michigan. Thus, the Midwest discussed here overreflects the agricultural Midwest rather than the industrial Midwest.

Table 6.3 **Differences among Selected Candidate Activities by Region**

Activities Undertaken*		Northeast	Midatlantic	Southeast	Midwest	Southwest	Mountain	Pacific
Visiting factories and/or gates		26.7%**	22.3%	25.6%	8.4%	18.1%	9.6%	1.9%
Visiting shopping centers		53.1%	44.4%	34.1%	28.3%	50.0%	28.6%	28.3%
Door-to-door campaigning		26.7%	34.3%	34.1%	38.3%	40.9%	38.0%	50.9%
Attending political party functions		40.0%	28.0%	31.8%	35.0%	27.2%	33.3%	31.1%
	N =	15	36	43	60	22	21	53

(N = 250)
  *See question III.12 on the questionnaire in appendix I for the exact wording of the question and answers.
  **Cell entries are percentage of candidates in each region responding that they engaged in the activity ''nearly every day'' or ''many times a week.''

less frequently visited by candidates. However, door-to-door campaigning is more frequently used, particularly on the West Coast. Though the differences are not so large, political party functions are most frequently a part of campaigns in the Northeast, least frequently in the Southwest. This disparity accurately reflects historical strengths of the parties in those sections of the country.

The data do not reveal that winners are distinguished from losers by campaign activities. If one eliminates those candidates who campaigned little at all, all of whom lost their primaries, no activity was engaged in much more by winners than by losers; nor more by losers than by winners. Districts differ; candidates differ. What is right for one candidate in one district might not maximize the votes for another candidate in that district nor for the same candidate in another district. One of the most frequent errors by candidates is to attempt to replicate someone else's campaign. As mentioned earlier, primary campaigning is more art than science. The art in this case is to make the best possible use of a particular candidate's talents in a particular district at a particular time. Success in that endeavor, not the application of a magic campaign formula, distinguishes winners from losers.

USE OF FINANCIAL RESOURCES

The differences among primary campaigns in terms of financial resources available are of far greater magnitude than those relating to personal time. Campaign budgets in 1978 ran from a few hundred dollars to several hundred thousand dollars. These differences reflected seriousness of campaign effort, personal wealth of candidates, candidates' ability to raise money, and variations among districts. This last factor is particularly important if one examines the media outlets available in different districts. In some cases one or two television markets blanket the district and beam their signals to few places outside the district. In those cases, which tend to be more rural districts, television advertising is all but essential and frequently is not overly expensive. In other cases, the district falls entirely within one television market, but the same television signals cover many congressional districts; in these typically urban situations, television advertising is not cost efficient and is often prohibitively expensive. In still other districts, to reach the entire electorate a campaign would need to advertise in many television markets, none of which concentrates on the congressional district. Whether advertising rates are high or low, much of the money spent is wasted on voters concerned with other races. The same analysis can be made for radio and print media.

The amount of money to be spent on paid media advertising is the first variable one must consider in determining how a campaign budget is to be allocated. A campaign can ''nickel and dime'' some expenses, but if paid media are to be used, design and production costs as well as the actual cost of advertising time are not inconsequential. A decision to use paid media advertising involves a commitment to put hard money on the line, up front. Radio and television stations are prohibited from extending credit to political campaigns; production costs involve professionals' time and expensive materials. Volunteer efforts are often counterproductive, because an amateurish advertisement can convey a poor image that might well be worse than no such effort at all. Therefore, once a candidate has some clear idea of how much money will be available to be spent, he or she must decide whether or not to go the route of media advertising. For serious campaigns this decision is often dictated by the media markets accessible to the campaign, by the history of campaign efforts in the district, and by the probability that other candidates will follow this route.

As an unknown candidate facing at least one opponent who was likely to spend heavily on media in a district well-suited for such a campaign, I felt strongly that I would have to mount an extensive radio and television effort. However, as with so much else in this campaign, when I started I did not really appreciate what that commitment meant. In a preliminary budget I allocated half of my available financial resources to media advertising. In retrospect I know I pulled that figure out of thin air. I did not know production costs or advertising rates. I did not think through how much I would use radio, television, dailies, or weeklies. I had no idea of how many different spots I would use, nor how they should be integrated with the rest of my campaign. My ignorance was overwhelming, especially in light of the fact that I had worked on this aspect of other campaigns. Costs were escalating so quickly as to make earlier experience all but useless.

Bill Hamilton advised me to use an advertising agency that specialized in political campaigns. Instinctively I knew he was correct. I can recall no campaign in Maine, with the possible exception of former Governor James Longley's, in which the quality of media advertisements was up to the standard I had seen in New York and elsewhere. However, I soon discovered that "national political" firms had priced themselves out of the range available to all but the most expensive congressional campaigns. I could not justify spending half of my media "budget," undefined as it still was, for the consultive services of a large firm before I had even begun to pay for production or air time. I am still uncertain if I was right or wrong in that judgment.

As I mentioned earlier, I know I was wrong in my next step, taking the halfway measure of hiring a smaller, less experienced group from Boston. They were somewhat less expensive than the national firms, but still expensive. The principals involved were full of ideas but very weak on follow-through. Their experience was limited to one geographic area; they were incapable of translating that to rural Maine.

All along I knew I wanted a local firm involved in my advertising because I felt it would know the market better and because I wanted to avoid giving more fodder to those who were intent on branding me as an out-of-stater. After unproductive initial floundering that ate up too much of my budget, I turned over all of my advertising to the Camden-based firm of Duffy, Darrow, and Baer.

My experience in this area appears to be quite typical. Only slightly more than one-quarter of those responding to my questionnaire hired advertising firms to help in their campaigns at all; however, this percentage is explained by the fact that only 11.9 percent of those spending less than $25,000 (and only 4 percent of those spending less than $5,000) did so. Nearly three out of five of those spending over $50,000 did so. Of those who did hire advertising firms, 85.7 percent used local firms; 72.9 percent hired firms that were not primarily engaged in political work. Some of those running very expensive campaigns, with budgets over $100,000, were able to retain the national firms that specialize in political advertising; but very few others did so.

George Duffy, who personally handled my campaign for his firm, was very clear about his goals in this campaign and about my options. There was no way in which a campaign with my proposed budget could be a big moneymaker for him. However, success in this effort could put him in the forefront of those firms that dealt with Democratic candidates in Maine. He agreed with my assessment that no local firm had distinguished itself in this field. He also knew that success in the primary would lead to substantially more money in the general election. Thus, he had personal incentives that supplemented his commitment to my candidacy.

One reason that I settled on his firm was that he and I were politically compatible. Just as I had rejected Ad Media because of the political philosophy of the principal partners, George Duffy had decided against accepting other candidates because he did not believe in what they stood for. Duffy had come to Maine years before from Minnesota. His political roots were in the Humphrey-Mondale tradition of liberal Democrats. We spoke the same political language.

In addition, he quickly outlined what I could and could not expect him to do within the confines of my budget. Media blitzes were out; radio would be used heavily because it was less expensive and less often exploited by political campaigns. All of our efforts would revolve around a coordinated theme. Television would be used to introduce a theme that would be reinforced through other media. Duffy accepted my budgetary limitations and my commitment not to overextend my own financial resources. He demonstrated a concern for me as an individual that was most gratifying.

My media theme sought to challenge the electorate to get to know me. Our early commercials introduced me and a few of my ideas, the need to bring more jobs to Maine, the need for national health insurance, the need to reform the Congress.[2] They ended with the tagline, "When you know Sandy Maisel, you'll want him in Congress." My printed literature carried the same message. During the last three weeks, we ran three separate ads, one on Maine's economy generally, one on ideas for bringing jobs to Maine, one on my experience in Washington. Each of these ended with the line, "Sandy Maisel, you can put him in Congress." Finally, in the last week we switched to a tagline, "Now that you know Sandy Maisel, you can put him in Congress." In addition, we ran ten-second spots that acknowledged my underdog role: "I started this campaign as an unknown underdog. But because I've been talking about issues and listening to your views, I've been gaining your support. Now I need your vote on Tuesday."

All of the radio spots used the same script as the television commericals. The theory was to increase name recognition, to build a positive image, to build a personal line between me and the voter, and to give the impression of building momentum. The theory was excellent. I think the commercials were well received. But theory and a good critical response do not cast votes.

My commercials were run on all stations in the Portland market and on the one station in Bangor whose signal was strong enough to penetrate much of the district. Throughout the campaign we ran thirty-second commercials; in the last week we ran ten-second spots that paralleled the

2. Commercial scripts appear in appendix II.

longer commercials. We hit every radio market in the district, using ten-second spots much more frequently. I was frustrated with how little information one could get across in such short time spans, a reaction shared by others who ran campaigns based on issues.

Nationally, only about one-third of the primary candidates I surveyed used television at all. However, almost 60 percent of those spending over $25,000 used television. Regionally, candidates in the Southwest (72.7 percent) were most likely to use television. Those in the Midatlantic states (16.2 percent) and the Pacific Coast states (24.5 percent) were least likely. Based on this factors, winners could not be distinguished from losers. Those who did use television tended to rely on two or three 30-second spots. Fewer than 20 percent of those using television advertising used either ten-second spots or commercials of one minute or longer. Most candidates using television advertised on all stations that beamed to significant portions of their districts. The median cost for buying television time was approximately $8,000 for those who bought any time. Those who spent much more on their campaign spent much more on television. However, even among the more expensive campaigns, television expenditures of over $25,000 were rare. As a percentage of total expenditures, those spending between $25,000 and $100,000 budgeted most heavily toward television, with the mean being 20 percent of total budget. For more expensive campaigns the television expenditures did not rise proportionally, with the mean percentage falling to 12 percent.

Many more campaigns used radio advertising than television. Just under half of all respondents answered that they did use radio. Again, most used two or three different thirty-second commericals. About a third of those using radio also recorded one-minute advertisements. None used commercials longer than that. While the mean number of stations used for radio campaigns was six, 14 percent reported that their commericals were aired on more than twenty different stations. The mean amount spent on radio advertising was $4,000, again with more spent by the more expensive campaigns. The amount spent on radio constituted between 5 and 6 percent of the campaign budget, regardless of how expensive the total campaign was. One should note as well that radio production costs are all but negligible, while television production can easily cost over $1,000 for a thirty-second commercial. Again, regional differences are worthy of note. Nearly three-quarters of the campaigns in the Northeast and Southwest used radio advertising; fewer than half of those in the Midatlantic states and the Midwest and only one-third of those in the Pacific states did so. These differences do not reflect costs of campaigning so much as differences in campaign style.

Newspaper advertising was used by 73.9 percent of those responding to my questionnaire. Of those who used newspapers, 65.2 percent used both daily and weekly papers; 21.0 percent just weeklies; 13.8 percent, just dailies. Those in the Pacific states were much less likely to use this medium (53.8 percent) than those in other regions. Those in the Southeast and the Midwest relied far more heavily on weekly papers than did those in other regions. The mean amount spent on advertising in newspapers was around $4,500; as a percentage of the total campaign budget, those campaigns spending under $5,000 used only about 6 percent on newspaper advertising, while more expensive campaigns spent 9 to 10 percent.

Two less obvious forms of paid advertising were also used extensively in congressional primaries in 1978. Over a quarter of those responding used either billboards or public transit advertising. Many more campaigns used these in the Southwest (45.5 percent) and fewer in the Midwest (13.2 percent) than in the other regions. Nearly 60 percent of those spending over $50,000 used this type of advertising; only one out of six campaigns spending less than that amount used this medium. Those who employed this medium tended to invest heavily in it. One campaign spent over $25,000; on the average, the more expensive campaigns spent 10 percent of their budgets in this way.

Billboards are one form of advertising that appears to have ideological implications. Environmentalists campaign to rid the roadsides of eyesores. In Vermont, billboards are not permitted. Maine is working toward that goal. I personally decided not to use this form of advertising at all. That decision led Sue Kenyon, my campaign manager, to the most embarrassing moment she faced in the campaign. Unbeknownst to her, one of my local organizers owned a company that leased billboard advertising. One day he called the office and asked her when I was going to lease some of his billboards. He said he had been saving key spots for me. She replied that I did not believe in billboards, that I thought they should all be removed. Exit one campaign worker. Ad Media quickly tied down those billboards for Guy Marcotte.

While most of those I interviewed did not mention specific advertising media at all, two or three who used billboard advertising were extremely pleased with the results. As an example, Gene Salamon, in Illinois's Tenth District, bubbled with enthusiasm over this aspect of his campaign: "We isolated every billboard possible. We were on every North Shore bus and train. Commuters had to be aware of me as they went to work." I had a similar experience in the reverse. Dick Spencer's signs were on the back of every bus in Portland for two months. I felt he had won another important psychological battle because I could not campaign in Portland without seeing his name everywhere and knowing all of the voters were seeing it as well. However, his advantage lost out to exhaust fumes. After two or three weeks all of the signs were covered with dust. Joe Brennan, who had leased the fronts of the buses, fared much better.

Direct-mail advertising has become very important in national campaigns. This medium has begun to have an effect in congressional campaigns as well; 61.8 percent of my respondents did some direct mail advertising. Of those, 34.3 percent used district-wide mailings, while the others restricted themselves to selected lists. Again the cost of the campaign was the determining factor in using this medium, 80 percent of those spending over $50,000 advertised through the mail, most of those using district-wide mailings. Mailings seemed to be particularly effective in campaigns in which the other candidates ignored this approach. A Pennsylvania primary winner commented: "One of the main things I did was a big mailing. I determined that there wouldn't be a mailing for the other congressional candidates. I didn't think mine would be lost because they wouldn't be deluged."

If direct-mail advertising is done professionally, it can be very expensive and very effective. Lists must be purchased; slick letters are generated on computers; mail is sent first class. This medium is often effective at generating additional revenue as well as voter support. Campaigns with fewer financial resources are often in a catch-22-type situation. Their direct mail appeals are done by amateurs. The lists are incomplete; the letters are not personalized; the addressing is done by volunteers, and many envelopes are never completed. To save money, mailings are sent out bulk rate. They often are lost in the deluge of junk mail reaching most homes. This means of reaching voters so clearly favors campaigns with more financial resources that it might be well worth avoiding for those campaigns that cannot engage professionals to handle it.

Even in this age of modern media-oriented campaigns, even with sophisticated means of reaching large numbers of potential voters all at once, candidates and campaigns need the "memorabilia" of politics, the buttons, bumper stickers, road signs, handcards, gimmicks. Nearly every campaign uses some of these items. Campaign workers want and need them. How else can they show allegiance? How else can they feel that they are not alone, that there are others who are working for their candidate as well?

Almost everyone I have talked to feels that these items are necessary but not effective. The goal is to find the critically minimum amount needed, the amount that will make workers happy but will not cost too much. Few find this amount. The mean amount spent on items such as these was slightly over $4,000. However, all campaigns had to find a certain minimal amount to spend. For less expensive campaigns, that minimum amount constituted a high percentage of the total campaign budget, an average of 20 percent for those campaigns with budgets under $5,000; 27 percent for those with budgets between $5,000 and $25,000. While more expensive campaigns spent more on these items in absolute terms, the expenditures represented a much lower percentage of the total. The total picture that emerges from these data shows that those candidates who spend least on their primary campaigns spend the highest percentage of their budgets on the least effective means of appeal, campaign bric-a-brac; and they spend the lowest percentage on the most effective media, television and direct mail. Perhaps there is some higher logic at work in these allocations of campaign funds. Those who spend the least on their campaigns are also least likely to win. Losers want to have something by which to remember a campaign. One can remember funny incidents, personal contacts, stands of principle. However, all that one takes from a campaign of a tangible nature is leftover campaign material. One of my most dedicated volunteers arranged a collage of my campaign memorabilia. Making the collage was therapy for her; viewing it remains therapy for me. I am certain that many other losers frequently open the drawer filled with campaign clutter and think back on what might have been. In fact, there was little chance that it might have been; so expenditures on campaign memorabilia might in the long run be money well spent.

The more important question, of course, deals with how money was spent by those who had a significant chance of winning. I have tried to emphasize that how money is spent varies from district to district. If a common theme pervades, it is a cynicism toward the voters. One of those I interviewed talked about reaching the voters with an appeal to their intellect: "Educating the voters really did me some good. I sent out this brochure all over the district, and it really helped." But that (losing) candidate was a lonely voice in a chorus of those saying that to win one must use a lowest-common-denominator mass appeal.

> In Tennessee: This was a media campaign. There was no need to do anything else. . . . We didn't build any organization. . . . Nothing.

> In Pennsylvania: Next time I'd go real heavy on the media. Name recognition's number one. That's all the voter really knows.

> In Texas: Next time it'll just be television, pictures of Eckhardt and me. To hell with issues. . . . You can do a job on Eckhardt like Bentsen did on Yarborough in 1970 — you know the hippies on the Lincoln Memorial bit. You don't want to, but you have to to win.

The appropriate means to reach the voter varies with the nature of the district—television, radio, direct mail, billboards, door-to-door, phonebanks all work in some areas. The key for a successful campaign is to find the means that distinguish one candidate from the others. Except in very rare instances, issues do not play this role. More expensive campaigns use a larger variety of appeals, reaching the voters more frequently in more ways. Generally they do not win the voters over to the superiority of their candidate. Rather, they reinforce an image that media experts choose as one likely to have an appeal. In contested primaries there is no necessity that this image convert into one that will be successful in a competitive general election. In no case is a link established between a winning image and competence as a member of Congress.

USE OF FREE MEDIA

Candidates view the news media as an opportunity to get their message across to the public at no, or very little, cost. But what should the role of the media be in congressional primaries? If one can identify the appropriate role, one can next ask how well it is played.

Incumbents generally win in congressional elections, according to the latest evidence from political scientists, in part at least because of the weakness of those challenging them. Elsewhere I have examined this phenomenon to see whether the weakest challengers emerge from contested primaries or uncontested nominations. The press can note the weakness of challengers to incumbents, but surely the role of the press is not to recruit candidates. However, where contested primaries are in progress, the news media do have a responsibility. Their responsibility is to examine the candidates, to contrast them, to set the standard against which the people should measure those seeking their votes. The press's role should certainly not be that of a mere mouthpiece for candidates. The press should ask the questions citizens have a right to have answered. The press should intervene into the electoral process so that citizens can judge who in fact would be the best candidate and member of Congress.

The press does not play this role well. That failing is understandable given the role news media play in congressional districts. Just as the boundaries of other governmental units rarely parallel those of congressional districts, neither do those of media markets. In some cases many congressional districts are within one media market. The New York City news media cannot possibly give adequate coverage to all of those districts in New York, New Jersey, and Connecticut that they serve. No room or time would remain for coverage of anything else. At the other extreme, some congressional districts fall into a number of media-markets. These tend to be smaller media markets. While congressional candidates are more important to the news journalists in these areas, news staffs tend to be quite small. News coverage tends to center on local politics, to which newscasters and viewers can more easily relate. Congressional campaigns only get coverage when the candidates are easily accessible to the journalists.

In 1978 in Maine the media were nonactive participants in the congressional primary. To varying degrees news outlets carried the stories that the candidates released. My campaign and Dick Spencer's issued more releases than did Quinn's or Marcotte's. We were not always successful in having stories reported, however, because the radio and television stations and the dailies did not want to appear prejudiced in our favor. The key to gaining coverage was to have stories run by the wire services. The two wire services were headquartered in the state house in Augusta. The bureau chiefs knew Spencer because of his service in the state legislature. My press secretary, Bob Duchesne, massaged the egos of the bureau chiefs for some time before my releases were reported adequately.

Local papers and weeklies generally ran the wire service copy unless we were campaigning in their immediate area. Then, particularly if I personally visited a newsroom, they would run a longer story with a local news peg. I made a concerted effort to do this throughout the state, visiting every newspaper and radio station regularly on my trips through the district.

Only the Portland papers had a political staff sufficiently large to do any political analysis. Their top reporters, John Lovell and Tom Atwell, moved freely throughout southern Maine, though they spent most of their time between Augusta and Portland. Lovell and Atwell kept careful tabs on our campaign. They viewed my claims and my opponents' with justifiable skepticism. Like us, they were uncertain how the campaign was actually going. Their analytical stories revealed this uncertainty, accurately depicting what each campaign was doing, what strengths and weaknesses existed, what claims were being made, and which of these were supported by independent evidence. Their reporting emphasized that the campaign could go to any of us; they were also forthright in discussing our strengths both as potential congressmen and as candidates. While they did not give the campaign as much coverage as I would have liked, the quality of their reporting was impressive.

The coverage that Lovell and Atwell gave our campaign contrasts markedly with the coverage given the gubernatorial primary being contested at the same time. In that case they clearly stated that Waterville Mayor "Spike" Carey was not a factor in that race. Their negative coverage of Carey's chances frustrated him and undoubtedly contributed to the public perception that he did not have a chance. However, by objective measures — available money, organization, visible support — their conclusions were justified. Carey's campaign never did catch hold. His activities were covered fairly; their analysis of his potential was proven accurate on primary day.

Television coverage of the congressional campaign was sporadic. The Portland stations covered my announcement and the two press conferences I had in their area. Occassionally they would ''read'' press releases, but this type of coverage was most unusual. The public television station carried an hour-long debate among the four of us. However, voters could not have known much about our primary if television had been their sole source of news. We monitored all stations carefully to be certain that coverage was equal. In the final analysis, it was equal but inadequate. The situation in Maine was not unlike that in the other areas I studied. The main role played by the media was to separate out fringe candidates from those who had a real chance of success. This role is particularly important in contests with large fields of candidates, like those in the Texas and Illinois districts described below.

People were somewhat turned off because there were so many of us, but the media quickly got it down to three people; they called us the Big 3. We got most of the press. Like if there was a big article, it would be mostly about us and our pictures would be in and then they'd just mention the other four.

As it comes down to the end, the press weeds out those candidates who can't win. If I do it again, I'll have to get my ideas across early to get their attention.

If the media do play the role of narrowing the field of contenders, how do they choose? Certainly few news staffs do sophisticated polling or even checking on candidate organizations. Rather, reporters go on reputation. This helps incumbents and others who have been officeholders: "What did Carney have because of incumbency? Money and the power of the press. Newspaper coverage was the hardest part of running against an incumbent." However, at least one incumbent, Democrat William Clay from St. Louis, felt that the newspapers' coverage of him aided his opponents: "I guess so many challenged me because the papers gave the impression I was vulnerable. Actually it's a combination of people, but mostly the *Globe* and the people in the business community who feel I'm too liberal." Clay feels that the way the papers cover him is unfair: "The media is totally against me. There was a total news blackout on CBS in St. Louis for two years. They'll never quote me on anything unless it deals with minorities." If the press was totally against Clay, somehow he turned that into an asset. Despite being challenged by six fellow Democrats, he won his primary with over 60 percent of the vote.

If candidates do not realize the potential of the press to ignore them, they may well be "weeded out" early in a campaign. It is difficult to overcome media assessment that one's campaign is a forlorn exercise. However, most serious candidates evolve a media strategy aimed at assuring that their efforts are taken seriously. John Cicco described the importance he gave to massaging the local press: "When I first came back here, the first thing I did was go around and meet the township and borough chairmen. They all tried to discourage me, said I'd be crushed.

Table 6.4   **Attendance at Candidates' Press Conferences***

	Always	Sometimes	Never
By Print Media	39.7%	35.2%	25.1%
By Radio Stations	27.9%	33.0%	39.1%
By Television Stations	21.8%	36.3%	41.9%

(N = 179)
*See question V.9.a. on the questionnaire in appendix I for the exact wording of the question and answers.

Then I went to all of the editors in the area and tried to meet them. Their reaction was good. They liked that I paid attention to them. And, you know, it was like two trucks coming down a narrow road at each other. They'd wave both of them on because it would be a good picture. They love a fight.'' Cicco did not care why he was going to be covered, just as long as he was being covered.

Nearly three-quarters of the candidates responding to my questionnaire held some press conferences during their campaigns. Of the 25.2 percent who held none, only ten, 4.2 percent of the total, won their campaigns. Those who did win tended to run more expensive campaigns, making up for a lack of free media with paid media. The mean number of press conferences held was three; however, 15 percent answered that they held ten or more. Those who held press conferences felt that they were either ''very effective'' (28.9 percent) or ''somewhat effective'' (44.4 percent) in attracting attention to their campaigns. As table 6.4 demonstrates, press conferences by candidates in congressional primaries did not receive the kind of media coverage candidates for more prestigious offices would expect.

Over 90 percent of the responding candidates issued press releases during the campaign. Most candidates issued releases either once a week (29.3 percent) or a couple of times a week (26.0 percent); 7.7 percent issued daily releases. The difficulty, as one candidate put it, was ''to break out of the press release to garbage can syndrome.'' Massaging the press, staging ''live events,'' and holding press conferences were techniques used to distinguish one candidate's releases from another's. However, as table 6.5 shows, these techniques were not sufficient to gain much coverage of the candidates' ideas.

Candidates, winners and losers, were not very positive about the role played by the local news media in their campaigns. Only 8.5 percent felt that the media had done an excellent job; 32.0 percent felt that they had done a poor job, 19.0 percent felt they had done only fair.

There were no public debates at all in the districts of 41.8 percent of those responding to my questionnaire. Television carried debates in only

Table 6.5   **Percentage Whose Press Releases Were Reported**
"Always" or "Frequently"*

	Wire Service	Dailies	Weeklies	Radio	Television
Early in Campaign	16.8%	35.9%	33.5%	30.3%	19.6%
In Last Month	14.9%	37.8%	39.5%	33.1%	21.4%
In Last Week	13.9%	38.1%	37.2%	34.0%	23.2%

(N = 215)
*See question V.10.a. on the questionnaire in appendix I for the exact wording of the question and answers.

about a quarter of the districts; radio in 42.0 percent.. Again, it is understandable that television stations would not carry debates between candidates. In large media markets, too many debates would be called for because of the number of primaries in the area. In some districts, so many candidates were running that meaningful debates would last many hours. In other districts, incumbents refused to debate. Vince Gilmartin explained why there were no televised debates in Youngstown, Ohio, despite a heated primary: "No, we didn't have any debates. The stations couldn't arrange any because Carney refused. Why should he debate? His only campaigning was labor endorsements, the papers, and paid staff. He didn't need us."

Many candidates were critical because they felt the press was unsophisticated. The press could cover obvious stories and they could sense a good headline, but they could not get at the more important differences among candidates on the issues that they would face in Congress. Two candidates who benefited from this coverage pointed toward the press's overreaction to stories of corruption in Congress. Congressman Norman Shumway eventually beat twenty-two-year incumbent John McFall in November, after McFall survived a tough primary: "The local newspaper was guilty of overkill on the Ethics Committee thing. I didn't win one county where that paper is widely read and I won all of the others. . . . People didn't fault him for Koreagate. They just thought that twenty-two years of him was enough."

Mark Cohen lost a primary to incumbent Joshua Eilberg, who in turn lost the November election: "Corruption was the big issue in this campaign because of the media coverage. The firing of David Marston was seen as a national issue so we had to play it up in Philadelphia."

Other camplaints about lack of media sophistication covered a wide gamut. For example, Elliot Ozment's opponents in Nashville felt his write-in campaign received too much press coverage: "Ozment decided to run a write-in campaign. They gave him a lot of publicity because they could understand what he was doing. They couldn't understand nuclear power; it was too complex.'' Ozment might not have been critical, but he agreed with the assessment provided above: ''I was treated very fairly by the press. I got $250,000 worth of publicity — free publicity — because of my battle to get on the ballot and my write-in campaign.''

Finally, some felt the press was incapable of relating to new ideas. Many felt that the press was one-sided: ''Most of the papers in this district are run by conservative Republicans with interest in the utilities. By and large I didn't get good coverage. There were some responsible papers, but not too many.''

Few question that the news media can play a crucial role in congressional primaries. The media weed out some candidates. They keep others alive through frequent mention. They can set the context for a campaign, fueling the idea that an upset is possible. At the congressional level, the news media generally work on a ''hunch'' level. Their coverage is not sophisticated. Candidates work hard to be certain that they receive equal treatment. Serious candidates realize that equal coverage in the press, that follows from candidate effort, gives increased credibility to their campaigns. Martin Frost felt that the newspapers played a pivotal role in his upset victory: ''The *Fort Worth Star Telegram* is a conservative paper but it's very responsible. Even though I'm liberal, they wanted to endorse me. They contacted the Dallas paper and said, ''We'll do it if you do.'' We reprinted the endorsements and mailed them throughout the whole district. Usually endorsements don't mean much but these did.'' The news media rarely have that significant an impact. Incumbency and financial resources are still more significant variables for dividing winners from losers. But a strategy for obtaining free media coverage remains an important part of an overall plan for a campaign.

Candidates set one goal early: win the primary. They determine their resources, build their organizations, start raising money, and set a strategy. They develop tactics to implement that strategy. Some stick to their original plan. Many more change tactics as the campaign progresses, going with what feels good, what works, what they have the workers to do, what they can afford. No magic formula separates winners from losers. What succeeds for one fails for another. What fails for one succeeds for another. Winners try many tactics and waste much of their effort. But they devote a significant enough effort to those tactics that reach the voting public and convince them. How they identify those tactics remains something of a mystery, yet another reminder that successful politics is still more art than science.

7.
CONGRESSIONAL PRIMARIES: A FINAL VIEW

A PERSONAL APPRAISAL

Walking down Congress Street on my way into my Portland headquarters three days before primary day, I came to the conclusion that I was not going to win the nomination. Feminists often talk about one striking event that brings home emotionally what they knew rationally, that sex discrimination affects them personally, not just others. In the same way, a two-minute walk was all that was needed to convince me that my childhood dream was not to be fulfilled. I walked amidst hundreds of shoppers, with a huge Maisel for Congress sign overhead, with volunteers working the street with campaign literature, with my everpresent bow tie prominently displayed; and no one stopped me to wish me good luck. In fact, I was not certain that anyone recognized me. Six months before an election such anonymity was acceptable, if frustrating; with the election on the immediate horizon, it was a clear sign.

I did not share my revelation with anyone. In a strange way what I felt or did had become irrelevant in the final days of the campaign. The campaign had taken on a momentum of its own. As I related earlier, the decision to run had both an emotional and a rational element; the emotional element dominated. The assessment of one's chances as an election approaches is multifaceted as well. A rational assessment might be possible if anyone in a district is conducting sophisticated polls. But that was not the case in my campaign. Media analysts and those of us involved in the process had no hard evidence on which to base a judgment. The lack of a compelling rational reason to concede contributed to my decision to give Susan Kenyon *carte blanche* to run up my debt as the campaign neared completion; I would like to think that my idealistic views toward those who had worked so hard for me would have led to the same decision, but I cannot know that definitely. Lack of conclusive evidence that I would lose meant I could not give up for want of a few thousand dollars.

Emotionally neither Susan nor I felt ''up'' as primary day neared. We were not willing to give up hope, but neither did we sense victory. We felt we had accomplished much of what we set out to do; but we did not have a sense that it had succeeded. The feeling was not one of despair, but not one of elation. Dick Spencer seemed buoyant in the last weeks. I thought he had reason to be optimistic. But none of us was emotionally ready to give up.

Much of a campaign's planning must aim at the last week, when voter attention is highest. We felt that many voters would be undecided going into the last week. We wanted to have an impact on them as they reached their final choice. We wanted their last impression of our race as they entered their polling place to be a positive view of my candidacy. Weeks of planning went into our last days' efforts. Every volunteer was mobilized. My family — my mother, sisters, brothers-in-law, nieces, and nephews — all came in from Buffalo. Former students and friends from around the country converged on Maine. Susan Kenyon and Dan Hoefle, who coordinated my Portland campaign, dealt with incredible logistical problems. Family and friends had to be fed, housed, and transported. More important, they had to be in the right place at the right time with the right material. For this final week there was ''an army of Maisel workers.'' Every factory gate was hit once more. All of the major factories were hit twice, the final time on Monday or the Tuesday of the election. Key neighborhoods were canvassed again. Thousands of phone calls were made. Every place where many people were known to gather had Maisel volunteers present.

In many ways I became just another volunteer during this last push. No more planning had to be done. No more decisions had to be made. We were all Indians; there were no more Chiefs. All involved in the campaign felt incredible exhilaration and excitement; we were all impressed with how much we were accomplishing. The campaign was highly visible, moreso on a districtwide basis than any campaign other than Joe Brennan's for governor. We were accomplishing our goals. No one minded the lack of sleep, the crazy work hours. Momentum was carrying us forward. None of those so involved had time to assess the impact of this frenetic activity. Neither did I, until I walked down Congress Street and no one recognized me. But my revelation that the election was indeed lost had little impact; I shared it with no one and continued at the same breakneck pace. The last week's campaigning was a surreal experience. I saw no need to connect my activity with the goal at which it was aimed.

We all continued at the same pace right through the afternoon shift changes on primary day. Other candidates relaxed on primary day; I could not sit still. I made one final sweep of the length of the district, covering the same course I had on the day I announced. Then I toured Waterville's polling places, ostensibly checking turnout, but really thanking those who were still working right to the last hours. Only in the late afternoon did I collapse. I knew I had to summon enough energy to see my friends through our ''victory party''; I was convinced the result would not be good and I wanted to help others accept that. The problem was that, while I knew rationally and emotionally that I was not going to win, somewhere deep inside of me a flame of hope still flickered. How could I help others accept something I was not quite ready to accept myself?

Months earlier Susan Kenyon and I had developed goals for each part of the district. They were based on the best analysis we could muster, but not on very hard data. We simply could not estimate either our strength or that of our opponents. We did not know what factors would determine primary voting behavior in an election like this one. Neither political scientists nor practitioners have been helpful in this regard. But we did have our estimates of our own needs. While the victory party geared up outside, we holed ourselves up in one room of the Waterville Howard Johnson Fenway, awaiting returns.

The early returns for Waterville and surrounding areas were favorable. I was polling over 50 percent of the vote in a four-person field. Spencer was running second, but the others trailed badly. Allan Kleban, who all but single-handedly ran one coastal county and part of another for me, called in with encouraging returns as well. But the districtwide returns coming in on the radio were more realistic. We did not know what areas were reporting, but I was running third. The totals were close. Spencer held a slight lead; surprisingly, John Quinn was running second. In the gubernatorial race, Joe Brennan's victory seemed assured; ''Spike'' Carey, whose supporters were awaiting results at a hotel across the street, was running a distant third.

As soon as the returns for the Portland area came in, a clearer picture emerged. I was running very poorly throughout all of Cumberland County. Quinn was outdistancing all of us, capturing a clear majority in many areas, taking the district lead from Spencer. As York County began to come in with its strong support for Marcotte, I slipped into fourth place. Marcotte challenged and eventually passed Spencer. Quinn's lead grew and seemed insurmountable. I knew it was time to concede. I spent some time alone preparing my remarks and then a few moments with Susan Kenyon, mostly thanking her and assuring myself that she was ready to face the others.

The ovation I received as I was about to concede defeat is something I will never forget. I was composed and ready to be most gracious to John Quinn. Then I spotted Joy Vigue, the high-school student who had worked endless hours on my behalf. She truly "believed" in me in a most irrational way. She was devastated that I had lost and was crying uncontrollably. I went over and held her; the tears flowed down my cheeks as well. I gave an abbreviated speech. Very few who worked so hard on the campaign held in their emotions. There is something quite healthy about a group cathartic experience. The rest of the evening was spent thanking people and reminiscing. Very little time was spent on analysis. I talked to John Quinn and Dick Spencer, but the conversations were perfunctory. In many ways the evening was one big deep breath.

The next morning the letdown really set in. We had forty-eight hours to clean out two campaign headquarters or face additional rent charges. No one felt up to the task; but everyone pitched in. Records were packed away, some for storage, others to be sent to Quinn's headquarters. Extra campaign material was thrown out. Mementos were saved. Mostly we sat around and picked up the pieces. Who had what plans for the summer? Did people need help securing jobs at so late a date? What role would we play in the fall campaign? Kevin and Nancy Hill came through in our time of defeat as they had throughout the campaign. That night they threw a huge party at their home. That was the time we could all let our hair down together. A group of people who work hard for a goal for months on end need a time to crash together. If anyone remained sober that night, I would be the last to remember. The evening was a time of sharing feelings about good friends and for putting one aspect of one's life behind as a new one started.

I had planned to vacation for the two weeks after the primary, whether I won or lost. As it turned out, my vacation was extended. We decided to go to England, to spend some quiet time in the countryside with good friends who were themselves renting a cottage south of Oxford. However, three weeks passed between the end of my campaign and our trip to England.

Those were very important weeks for me. First, it was a time to relax, to go to the beach with my children, to readjust to a normal daily schedule, to read Robert Ludlum. Life as a candidate is far from normal. Readjustment to the world as others live it is not an easy process.

Second, during those weeks I had a chance to look at the election results in some detail. I wanted to know in a precise way why and where I had lost. This analysis was revealing. For a time Georgia nominated candidates for office on the basis of county units. The nominee was that candidate who carried the most counties in a district. That system, which clearly violates the one person-one vote principle, has long been abandoned. I wished for its return, as I had won pluralities in three of the seven counties, Kennebec and the coastal counties of Knox and Waldo, where my campaign, run by Allan Kleban, had been the only campaign put on by any congressional candidate. Spencer had won the other two coastal counties; Marcotte had won York County; Quinn had won Cumberland.

Quinn ran a close second to me in Kennebec, because he carried the Augusta area impressively. Spencer was my nearest competition in Knox and Waldo. He also ran reasonably well in the rest of the district. However, Quinn's margin in the Portland area alone proved to be enough to gain the victory. Marcotte finished second because he carried Biddeford, Saco, and Sanford, the population centers in York County, by very wide margins, with the rest of us running quite close together.

A clear pattern emerged, a pattern that V. O. Key (1949) identified in his classic *Southern Politics* as "friends-and-neighbors" politics. Each of us won in those areas where we were best known, where our names were most familiar. In my case that was also the area where I was able to organize the most successfully. Quinn and Marcotte never really developed organizations of the type Spencer and I had. However, Quinn in Portland and Marcotte in York County piggybacked on the Brennan campaign. The correlations between Quinn's votes and Brennan's in the Irish area of Portland are especially noteworthy. Where none of us could draw on "friends and neighbors," organization made the difference. Mine was the only organization in Waldo County; it was the best in Knox. Spencer's was by far the best in Lincoln and Sagadohoc counties and in the smaller towns in Cumberland that he carried.

None of these conclusions should have been very surprising. In fact, contrary to my assertion earlier, political scientists have given an analysis on which we could have drawn. However, it was difficult to see beforehand how that analysis was relevant. After all, we are now in an age of "new politics." Three of us ran extensive media campaigns, though Spencer's and Marcotte's far outdistanced mine. Why were these not decisive? What was their impact?

Again, answers do appear. Congressional primaries are low salience elections, especially when a major office is contested at the same time. Our media campaign served to increase public awareness of our candidacies. Quinn had had a tremendous name recognition advantage because of his much publicized career as the state's consumer advocate. He and his family were also very well known in the largest Democratic area in the district. None of the media campaigns caught the public's fancy. None was successful in creating an instant celebrity. Consequently, no one came out of the "new politics" aspect of this campaign with an advantage. If only one of us had been able to use the electronic media, or if one of us had used it much more successfully than the others, the result might well have been different.

As it was, the result followed from "old," not "new," politics. Who had the best organization? Who could mobilize his own constituency? In a four-person field, I should have foreseen that I was beaten under these circumstances. Where I could put an organization together and in my own geographic constituency, I won. However, I never successfully matched Spencer's organization in areas where he was strong. Further, my geographic base was the smallest of the four. If I could have mobilized a strong liberal-issue clientele, then winning might still have been possible. However, Spencer and Quinn had legitimate claims on liberals as well. I am quite certain that those farthest to the left on social and economic issues favored me, but the portion of the ideological spectrum to which I had sole claim was clearly too small to create a winning coalition.

Quinn won because of his geopraphic base, or more precisely becasue of his two geographic bases. He did very well in the Portland area and the Augusta area, where he lived for a number of years and where his wife's family resides. He undoubtedly pulled well from consumer activists as well, but that was a small group. I do not believe that Quinn ever understood the significance of his primary victory. He never successfully penetrated any of the areas in the general election in that he had done poorly in the primary.

The election was most frustrating for Dick Spencer. He alone had planned a political career some years in advance that was to culminate in this election. He was supremely confident that he could beat me one-on-one, a confidence that I still question. He was also confident right up until primary day that he would win the four-way race. His organization was stronger in more places than were the others. But each of us sniped at his support. Marcotte took all of his support in York County, a constituency he had worked on for some time. Quinn destroyed his campaign in the Portland area, despite the fact that Spencer was well known and respected in the legal and political communities there. I undercut his base among liberal Democrats. Spencer feels today that my candidacy beat him. I think he is wrong. Had I not been in the race, my votes would not have gone disproportionately to any one candidate. Spencer's organization was strongest in my home area, but Quinn and Marcotte could easily have made appeals to pockets of potential supporters. In many ways they wrote off this area because of my strength.

Finally, Marcotte's strategy nearly succeeded. He held his geographic base. He made inroads in other areas because of his "tough guy" media campaign and his direct appeal to Franco-American voters. He lost because he was not an individual to be taken seriously. If he had been seen as a person of substance, his media campaign might have been enough to offset "friends-and-neighbors" loyalty. However, his appeal was heavy-handed and essentially ineffectual. Ad Media failed in its attempt to create a candidate to fit the image it wished to portray.

In drawing these conclusions in the weeks after my primary, I was struck by how unique the situation in this district was. This kind of analysis could not have been done without a detailed knowledge of the district, the candidates, and their campaigns. That is the key lesson. The answer to the question "Can a young, Jewish college professor from Buffalo win in a district such as this one?" is, "It depends." Similarly, if one asks, "What are the determinants of voter behavior in congressional primaries?" the answer is, "It depends." Each district is different, each political environment is different, each campaign is different. Generalization about the impact of "new politics," "old politics," "friends-and-neighbors politics" or any other brand of politics fails. Clem (1976: 6-13) lists fourteen variables that one should isolate in examining congressional campaigns. The combinations of these variables lead to the diversity of campaign experiences. Particular circumstances, not general guidelines, determine who wins those elections that are hotly contested. Other than pointing to the advantages of incumbents, who rarely face serious challengers, one cannot successfully draw broad conclusions.

In addition to readjusting to a normal life-style and analyzing my own defeat, I used the weeks immediately after the primary to reflect on my participation in the electoral process. My friends were most supportive, urging me not to be disappointed, to try again. I reached a different conclusion. While the experience of running for office was personally enriching and one I will never regret, I also knew immediately that I would never again seek election. I reached this conclusion for two reasons.

First, the personal costs were too high. During the six months of my campaign, despite sincere efforts to avoid such action, I gave up all other aspects of my personal life to reach one goal. When I was with my family and friends, I was constantly preoccupied. When I met new people, I viewed them only in political terms. I was unable to focus on anything other than politics. Holding a congressional seat means maintaining that level of personal commitment. The voters demand it; one's sense of self-preservation in office calls for it; continued success requires it. I am not that dedicated, nor do I want to be.

Ironically, the second reason is related to the first: I liked campaigning too much to ever do it again. The most enjoyable part of campaigning is seeing new places and meeting new people, different people from those I meet in my everyday life as a college professor and active citizen. I learned a great deal about Maine, about what Maine citizens do for work, about their concerns, fears, hopes. I thrived on the give-and-take of political debate, on learning about issues that confront the state and the nation, on demonstrating my mastery of these. All of these aspects of campaigning weigh in on the positive side.

However, I also had a taste of the aphrodisiacal appeal of power. Others' lives revolved around mine. Others cared what I said, what I did. They looked after my schedule, drove me from place to place, provided for my every need. Someone was always at my beck and call, to do whatever I said needed to be done. I found that appalling at first, but I quickly became used to it. In the final analysis, I found that to be frightening. I am not that important; I have seen too many politicians who feel that they are. I came away from the campaign uncertain that I could resist that temptation. I saw the type of individual I was becoming and rejected that person. If I was unable to resist that temptation as a candidate, how much easier would it be for me to submit as an office-holder? If I did so, I would be no better than those in office I frequently criticize. That path is not for me.

My friends and my family stuck by me throughout my campaign and after it. For that I am most grateful. I am certain their patience was frequently tried. The normal life-style I desire seems incompatible with a career in electoral politics. I prefer the former to the latter. Thus, in many ways my electoral defeat is not regrettable. Like many others who run for office and lose, I am not unhappy to return to the public obscurity from which I came.

Most of those losers I interviewed and most who answered the questionnaire shared my view, particularly of the positive aspects of the campaign experience. Over half replied that running for office was a ''very beneficial personal experience.'' Over half responded that they would probably run for office again sometime, nearly one-third in 1980. However, 40.9 percent felt that campaigning had ''many good aspects, but high personal costs.'' Another 8.7 percent answered that the ''personal costs [were] too high.'' About one-third commented that it was unlikely they would ever seek political office again or they definitely would not. Looking more deeply into these data, it appears that those losers who already held or had run for public office were most likely to seek office again. If history is to guide, it is likely that they will continue to be unsuccessful. Eventually, they will return to a level of office basically obscure to the public's eye or the voters will assign them to the political oblivion that many of the first-time office seekers choose themselves.

These observations suggest some more general issues that should be raised, even if they cannot be explored in depth. Essentially I concluded that I could not handle the job I sought; yet in many ways I still think I would have been a good member of Congress. How do those who are successful learn to cope with these concerns? Fenno (1978) details how members relate to their constituents. Some of those he followed seem to adapt quite well, while others seem to be constantly on the merry-go-round I experienced. Cooper and West (1981) discuss why more members have chosen early retirement in recent years. Certainly my feeling about the personal cost of seeking and holding office coincides with some of the reasons they identify. The House of Representatives is composed of an extremely diverse group of individuals, at different points in their careers, with different personal and family backgrounds, with different career objectives. That is the strength of the institution. That service in the House is not an appropriate career goal for someone who might have been a productive member is not an indictment of those who serve nor of the House. Rather, it reflects one constraint on the recruitment process that those exploring entrance into the House should take into account.

AN APPRAISAL OF PRIMARIES AS PART OF THE ELECTORAL PROCESS

It is not enough to look at the effect of primaries on personal careers. Most of the 962 candidates in 1978 did start from political obscurity; most did or will end up in political oblivion. However, 435 individuals, some candidates in contested primaries, many not, did end up as members of the Ninety-sixth Congress. What role did the primary process play in recruiting these candidates and in shaping the composition of that Congress?

Perhaps the most appropriate point of departure is a statement concerning the role primaries were meant to play. According to Robert M. LaFollette, whom many consider the father of the direct primary:

> Put aside the caucus and convention. They have been and will continue to be prostituted to the service of corrupt organizations. They answer no purpose further than to give respectable form to political robbery. Abolish the caucus and the convention. Go back to the first principles of democracy; go back to the people. Substitute for both the caucus and the convention a primary election . . . where the citizen may cast his vote directly to nominate the candidate of the party with which he affiliates. . . . The nomination of the party will not be the result of ''compromise'' or impulse, or evil design — the ''barrel'' and the machine — but the candidates of the majority, honestly and fairly nominated. (La Follette, 1913: 197-98)

In theory, direct primaries do take power from political ''bosses,'' whether they be powerful or not, and give that power to the people.

The question is whether the empirical reality matches the theoretical promise. In the case of congressional primaries, the answer seems to be that it does not.

First, two basic questions will be raised, though definitive answers cannot be given. We know little about the congressional nominating process before the advent of direct primaries. We do know that these nominations were closely controlled by political bosses in areas with dominant machines. Congressional seats tended to go to loyal followers who were willing to act in Congress as if they were a mere extension of the organization back home. But dominant political machines whose influence extended over many congressional districts were able to maintain control even after the advent of the primary system. When the Johnson administration needed votes from the Chicago delegation in the House, the liaison line from 1600 Pennsylvania Avenue to Capitol Hill detoured through Chicago. We have a less clear picture of how nominations were decided in those areas in that the congressional district covered a geographic area broader than that of most political organizations. We know that the process generally involved caucuses and congressional district conventions, but we are less certain, if we demand analytical rigor, who influenced these nominations, how, and why. The general perception seems to be that they were not highly prized by political organizations and thus the method of nomination used for congressional seats was not really the evil at which the primary was aimed.

Similarly, we do not have a firm grasp of the extent to which the "people" participate in congressional primaries. Primary turnout varies significantly from state to state and from district to district within the same state. Turnout in congressional primaries varies to some extent with the excitement generated by other primary elections held on the same day. Turnout varies with the competition present in the primary and in others held the same day. The major analytical problem in this area involves deciding what we should be measuring if we seek to determine the extent to which the "people" are involved in the nominating process.

What is clear, however, is that popular participation is meaningless if candidates run unopposed. Long ago, V. O. Key (1956) projected that the impact of the direct primary would be a weakening of local party organization, which in turn could lead to the demise of minority parties in many areas. One role of political parties is to assure that ballot positions are filled, that competition exists, so that the electorate has the opportunity to hold officeholders accountable by voting them (and their party) out of office. Key's concern was with the number of state legislative seats that were not contested.

The causal link between the advent of direct primaries and the demise of party organization is less clear at the congressional district level at which

Table 7.1 **Decline in Competition for House Seats**

PERCENTAGE OF SEATS WITH ONLY ONE
MAJOR-PARTY NOMINEE

	Presidential Year	*Off-Presidential Year*
1964	9.0%	
1966		10.8%
1968	10.1%	
1970		11.0%
1972	12.4%	
1974		13.6%
1976	11.7%	
1978		13.8%

formal party organization tends to be amorphous in any case. However, the lack of competition that Key observed is very much in evidence.

The existence of a presidential election has some impact on congressional races. Table 7.1 shows that in the 1960s only about one in ten House seats was not contested by both major parties. By the late 1970s, a different pattern emerged. Despite the fact that the Republicans were contesting many Southern seats that for years had gone automatically to the Democrats, the total number of seats not contested by one or the other of the major parties increased. Primary competition did exist in some of these districts (recall table 1.1). However, as we know little about either turnout or level of competition in those primaries, and as we have ample evidence that incumbents challenged in those primaries almost invariably win, political analysts interested in the electoral process have cause for concern. We know entirely too little about recruitment of congressional candidates. What we do know is that the recruitment system does not work well to guarantee the electorate some choice.[1]

What about those primaries that are contested? Again,the evaluation is not a positive one. As is the case with general elections, primary elections against incumbents are almost always futile. Over a third of the primaries held in 1978 involved incumbents. Only five incumbents lost those primaries; very few others were seriously challenged. The advantage of incumbency and the perception of that advantage by potentially strong challengers lead to electoral situations in which most incumbents need not worry about competition from within their own party.

Primary competition for congressional nominations is most significant

1. The issue of competition in congressional elections is an important one that merits further attention. If more seats are in fact won by default, political scientists should examine why this is so, in what regions, with what impact on the House.

in those districts in which the incumbent is viewed as vulnerable, a situation that often leads to stiff competition for the nomination to run against the incumbent, and in those districts in which no incumbent is seeking reelection, a situation that often leads to competitive races in both parties unless the district is thought to be safe for one party (again, refer to table 1.1). Even in those districts, however, the process is flawed. One of the major problems noted throughout this analysis has been the presence of a large number of candidates who have no chance of gaining success but who "muddle" the voters' minds nonetheless. State election laws either encourage or discourage such candidates. In Tennessee, an example referred to earlier, only twenty-five signatures are needed to secure a place on the ballot. In Pennsylvsnia and elsewhere, individuals can be candidates in primaries for more than one office at the same time. Other states have much more restrictive procedures.

The dilemma here is between, on the one hand, assuring ballot access to all candidates who are serious about running and can have an impact on the election and, on the other hand, keeping "frivolous" candidates who only serve to confuse the electorate off the ballot. How open should the system be? If one tries to exclude some candidates, does one unduly restrict the democratic process? Each state must answer these questions within the framework of its unique political culture. What seems clear from this analysis of experiences throughout the nation, however, is that few state lawmakers have examined the consequences of laws relating to ballot access.

Those I interviewed were uniformly in agreement on few matters. However, all of those competing in large primary fields, all of whom were running in states with permissive ballot-access laws, concurred that the size of the field had a detrimental effect on the electorate's ability to choose. Each candidate felt it important that the laws be changed to restrict ballot access to those who had some hope of attracting a significant following among the primary voters. There was no uniformity in solutions to this problem. Obviously, raising the number of signatures required is one technique. Reinvigorating political parties and a system of preprimary conventions to gain ballot access (with a signature petition option) seems another alternative. If the party organizations' role in congressional nomination were reinvigorated, as it is in states such as Connecticut, Delaware, and Virginia, fewer seats would go uncontested in the general election. However, if the rules were too restrictive, primary competition itself might disappear, as has happened to a large extent in the states mentioned above. The public policy objective here is to strike the appropriate balance between a role for political party organizations and domination by those organizations.

Those I interviewed were also nearly unanimous in their feeling that voter apathy about primaries constituted a serious problem. The primary process is, or should be, central to our electoral system. This process is the way we structure the choices that the voters face in November. But the voters seem to care little about this structuring. Many complain about the choices presented to them; others are satisfied to vote for the incumbent; few care about the process.

This apathy is frustrating for candidates. It is potentially dangerous for our political system. American citizens claim to be less and less satisfied with the performance of the Congress, but they are also unwilling to do anything about it (Fenno, 1975). Fenno's paradox can be extended. When President Carter came down from his retreat to Camp David and proclaimed that the country was suffering from a malaise, he was justifiably criticized for not realizing that his lack of leadership caused that malaise. However, at another level, perhaps President Carter was right. Perhaps Fenno's paradox — that we as a country are frustrated by the performance of our Congress but praise the job done by our individual representatives in Congress — can be explained by a type of malaise, a malaise about the political process.

American citizens face a complicated, cumbersome, complex, and frequently unfruitful political process. They are asked to go to the polls over and over again. On the average, Americans vote six to eight times in a biennium, far more civic participation than is expected in any other advanced democracy. When they are not satisfied with the results produced by the government, frustration sets in. One result of this frustration is a type of malaise. Why should they bother participating? Turnout rates go down, to near 50 percent in presidential elections, much less in others. Interest in politics and identification with political parties decline.

This malaise is particularly evident in congressional primaries. The citizens do not think highly of the Congress. For the reason Fenno and others have pointed to, they are familiar, comfortable, and satisfied with their own representative, why should they bother to participate? Participation necessitates enrollment in a party, another trip to the polls, making a choice. What is the payoff? Besides, they will have to vote again in November. Result: apathy, malaise.

Can anything be done to reverse this situation? First, it is necessary to assert that something should be done. Continued frustration and apathy will lead to a system that continues to be unresponsive to the will of the people. Support from the system will continue to decline. Frustration with results will continue to build. If citizens disapprove of government action and feel they have no say in what happens, the system is ripe for exploitation by demagogues claiming the easy fix for complex problems. One crucial goal of our democratic process should be to avoid this situation by convincing citizens that their participation is important and meaningful.

The first step in reinvigorating our nominating system should be to simplify it. One means of simplifying the process is to make it more amenable to media attention. Most Americans now receive most of their political information from television. Television does not and probably cannot do an adequate job of covering congressional primaries as the system exists today. Media markets do not correspond to political districts. Not only is there the problem of some media markets covering many districts and of other districts spanning many markets, there is also the problem that results from the fact that television signals ignore state lines; as different states hold primaries at different times, political news is often irrelevant for many seeing a station's programming.

However, if all of the primaries in the nation, or perhaps all in a region, were held on the same day, the primary election would become a national — or regional — event of significance. Media coverage would focus the electorate's attention on politics much more than is possible now. For some time, reformers have talked of a national primary or system of regional primaries for delegates to the national nominating convention for president. Some regional primaries have evolved in recent years. There has been no groundswell of support for this reform, however, because such a system would obviously favor some potential candidates over others — those who are already well known, those with a base in the area of the first regional primary, as examples.

No such advantages would accrue to individual candidates if all congressional (and presumably senatorial) primaries were held on the same day. Incumbents might be slightly disadvantaged, because presumably the voters would be paying more attention to their opponents than is the case now; but incumbents have so many other advantages that this change seems minimal. The positive consequence of raising the public's awareness of these elections and its attentiveness to them would far outweigh any disadvantages.

The practical problems involved in moving all primaries to one day are much more significant than the theoretical ones. As states control the laws under which party primaries are run, such a reform would require either a constitutional amendment, the prospect for which seems remote given the low salience of this issue, or incredible cooperation and coordination among those state officials responsible for running elections. While such cooperation might be possible on a regional basis, the idea of extending it nationally seems a forelorn hope. Even regional cooperation involves concurrence on when primaries should be held. The ''primary season'' now extends over a six-month period. Some states opt for early spring primaries; a few hold primaries in the summer; the rest wait until after Labor Day. Two factors determine the dates chosen. First, each state will argue that its date fits the peculiar circumstances of that state. For instance, Maine officials would argue that a spring primary is necessary because so many people are involved in vacation-industry-related employment, and so many out-of-staters populate Maine in the summer, that politics in the summer is unproductive. Second, politicians have differing views on the appropriate length of time from the end of the nominating process until the general election. Some argue that nomination should be determined as near to the November election as is possible, to reduce the amount of time spent campaigning. Others argue that a shorter general-election campaign works to the advantage of the incumbent, who is already well known, as opposed to the challenger, who must first unite his or her party, if it was split in the primary, and then build momentum toward the November election. To show the complexity of this issue, others argue that challengers are disadvantaged by early primaries, because they lose the momentum that a primary victory gives them.

No consensus exists at this time. Empirical studies could answer part of the question about who is advantaged by differing primary dates, but even sophisticated analysis will not put this question to rest in the minds of practitioners. Each will revert to the argument about the uniqueness of individual states to support positions that result from gut feelings. Breaking down existing patterns would not be easy; but that conclusion does not suggest that such an effort should be abandoned.

However, even if the process were simplified and more citizens were involved, a more basic problem would remain. Congressional primaries are not competitive. The advantages that accrue to incumbents discourage serious challengers from entering the fray. Nominations and in some cases elections go by default because thoughtful activists realize the futility of most contests.

Reformers have looked to campaign-finance legislation as a means to reduce the inequities that exist in congressional elections, primaries as much as general elections. However, the questions raised at the end of chapter 4 demonstrate the complexity of this issue. No easy answers appear.

For political scientists to attack this problem, more needs to be known. My study of primary contests around the country led me to conclude that most fields of candidates, regardless of their size, were exceedingly weak. In seeking to improve the primary process so that the electorate is presented with better choices, it is necessary to return to an examination of the decision to run. High-level government positions in the executive branch are often filled by prominent individuals who make themselves available to an administration of their political party and return to their positions in the private sector once government service is ended. The tradition of ''in-and-outers'' is an important one in our government's history.

Individuals of similar stature do not run for Congress. We know why people do run. We know much less about why others do not run. Considering the obscurity from which most congressional candidates come, it is small wonder — and little loss — that most end up in political oblivion. The loss is that congressional candidates do not come from those more prominent in their communities. The agenda for the years ahead is to examine nonrecruitment, to see why prominent individuals do not seek elective office, and then to determine how the system can be changed to attract those individuals as candidates, to reinvigorate the process by offering the electorate a choice among individuals whose stature and place in society is such as to inspire the confidence of the electorate.

President John Kennedy said: "In a democracy, every citizen, regardless of his interest in politics, 'holds office'; every one of us is in a position of responsibility; and, in the final anlaysis, the kind of government we get depends on how we fulfill those responsibilities." However, citizens cannot take these responsibilities seriously if they do not respect their political institutions. And they will not respect those institutions if they are not led by men and women of stature, fellow citizens willing to enter upon the perilous road of electoral politics in order to serve the public, men and women who heed President Kennedy's warning and look upon it as a challenge to be met.

Where else but in the political profession is the individual expected to sacrifice all — including his own career — for the national good?

POSTSCRIPT: 1984

A PERSONAL VIEW

A good deal has happened to me in the six years since I ran for Congress. Some of it reflects on that experience. More of it is truly personal. And that defines the difference.

As a candidate for Congress, and as an author writing about a congressional campaign, nothing was strictly personal. Candidates for public office — and their families — have less and less "space," to use the currently popular term than just about any other people in the public eye. Their every move is open to press inspection; their personal lives belong to the public as much as to themselves. And, as recent literature has shown, this has caused many to forego the experience of serving, or attempting to serve, in Congress (Cooper and West, 1981).

Shortly after my defeat, I decided that I would never seek public office again. I have never wavered from that determination. In the late summer after my June primary, the candidate for State Senate from my district resigned. I was asked to take the nomination and seek the seat. One of the arguments put forth was that a seat in the Senate would be a perfect jumping off point in another bid for Congress. I was not impressed. That argument might have meant more to me if I had my heart set on another run for Congress or if I had a strong desire to work on state issues. Neither of those feelings was present. I went back to teaching and writing.

But, one might ask, what is the role in politics of a "rising star," plunged back to oblivion at age thirty-three? If you recall my decision to run, you might recall that I spent some time with Gordon Weil, one of those whom politicos in Maine view as a *cognescenti*. Every potential candidate marched to Gordon Weil's door to hear political wisdom. Though a fairly young man, by virtue of his experience, Weil had become something of a senior statesman among Maine Democratic politicians.

Much to my surprise, the same role has fallen to me. Every two years those who are thinking of running for Congress in the First District of Maine call and ask if I will spend some time with them. I dutifully set aside that time, wondering what wisdom one who finished fourth in a four-way race can have. The candidates come, full of energy and hope. I ask them some basic questions: What is your base of support? Who is going to run your organization? How much money do you think the primary will cost? The general election? Where will you get the money? How far into debt are you willing to go? Why? Then I give them a copy of this book and tell them to read it carefully.

Mostly I have told these candidates not to run. In 1980 only one candidate, State Chairman Harold Pachios, a Portland attorney, sought the nomination. He was demolished by Emery. In 1982 Emery decided to run for the United States Senate seat to which George Mitchell had been appointed when Edmund Muskie became secretary of state. That seemed like a good move for Emery, as Mitchell had never won a statewide race. Emery's decision opened up the First District seat. The line of potential candidates trooped to my door. I gave out lots of free advice. Some of it was followed; some was ignored. That is as it should be. I even endorsed one candidate, spending a little time on his campaign. He lost. I also found out that I had no desire to have anything to do with active campaigning again. The thrill was gone; some of the pain remained.

Emery was succeeded by John McKernan, a young, attractive, intelligent, moderate Republican. He won the 1982 election over Democratic primary winner John Kerry. Kerry's campaign was badly hurt by the abortion issue. His pro-life stance, which helped him in the primary, cost him liberal Democratic support in the general election. Once again the Democrats had destroyed their own chances in Maine's First District.

And in 1984 two candidates sought my advice on whether they should seek the Democratic nomination to oppose McKernan. One was Barry Hobbins, the state party chair, who had succeeded Pachios. Hobbins, who also served in the legislature from York County, had played the party game well. He learned the lessons of Pachios' nomination and was well positioned to meet all challengers. It seemed to me that he had a lock on the nomination. It also seemed to me that he had no strategy for beating McKernan. I told him so; he didn't want to hear that.

Hobbins was challenged by Ralph Conant, the retired president of a small college in Unity, at one far corner of the district. Conant came to see me. I remember the conversation so clearly. I saw myself on a mission: "Save this guy from certain disaster." I told him that he would lose the primary badly, and that, even if he won the primary by some incredible fluke, he would lose the general election. He ran anyway. Hobbins beat him easily. Conant is a very bright man. His campaign never got off the ground. But I am not certain my advice to him was right. Since his primary defeat Conant has become more interested in the political process than ever before. I doubt he will run again, but a true activist has emerged. I suppose if he is not bitter, then the experience was worth it.

The speculation in Maine is that John McKernan will seek the gubernatorial nomination of the Republican party in 1986. The First District seat will be open again. I am certain that a large field will emerge. I'll not be in it. The six years since I have run have taught me a lot. David Brady's wonderful question, "Can a young, Jewish college professor win in a district like this one?" clearly deserves a "No" answer now. It probably did in 1978, or certainly after I reviewed my defeat, but only time can give the proper perspective. But that question really isn't the important one. The important one is "Would that young Jewish college professor trade the life he and his family have for the life of a member of Congress?" The answer to that is most definitely "No!" So, I have settled into what looks like a long career as a senior statesman. And the important personal things that have happened in my life? They remain just that — personal.

CONGRESSIONAL PRIMARIES: AN UPDATED APPRAISAL[1]

Part of my motivation for writing this book was that the political science profession had not looked very deeply into congressional primaries, that I and my professional colleagues had not done a very good job of preparing me, and others like me, for the electoral experience. The analysis in the chapters preceding this one tells a good deal about the 1978 congressional primaries. At the time those chapters were written, however, I had no way of knowing if 1978 was a typical year. Historical research would not have been very helpful in interpreting contemporary experience because

1. I am indebted to John Kramer for his assistance in gathering much of the data used in this section. One of the benefits of leaving politics and remaining in academia is the continued opportunity to work with the bright and talented young people with whom I am surrounded at Colby College. John and his fellow government students at Colby contribute significantly to my thinking about politics and my enthusiasm for ongoing research.

Table 8.1 **A Comparison of Congressional Candidacies, 1978-1984**

	1978	1980	1982	1984
Incumbent winners unopposed in both primary and general elections	43	37	35	43
Incumbent winners opposed in the primary, but not the general election	15	9	13	16
Opponents of these incumbents	22	13	16	22
Incumbent winners unopposed in the primary, but opposed in the general	204	223	207	211
Nominated to oppose these without contested primary	134	132	123	108
Nominated to oppose these with contested primary	70	91	84	103
Lost contested primary in these districts	109	159	142	164
Incumbent winner opposed in both primary and general elections	89	84	85	114
Lost primary to incumbent in these races	141	132	122	152
Nominated to oppose these without contested primary	45	36	49	64
Nominated to oppose these with contested primary	44	48	36	50
Lost primary to oppose incumbent in these districts	76	79	59	77
New member beat incumbent in general election after winning primary	14	15	16	7
Lost primary to eventual winner	34	22	30	18
Incumbent who lost was nominated without primary	10	8	12	4
Incumbent who lost had primary	4	7	4	3
Lost to incumbent who lost in general election	5	12	6	4
New member beat incumbent in primary and was unopposed in general	0	0	0	1
Losers to new member who beat incumbent in primary and was unopposed in general	0	0	0	2
New member nominated without primary and beat incumbent in general election	5	11	7	9
Incumbent who lost had no primary	3	7	7	6
Incumbent who lost had contested primary	2	4	0	3
Lost to incumbent who lost in general election	6	9	0	4
Open seat; new member had primary	49	38	49	22
Incumbent lost in primary to eventual new member	4	6	1	2
Incumbent lost in primary though new member in other party	1	0	0	0
Losers to new members in primary	149	126	136	72
Losers to new members in general; nominated without primary	20	10	15	4
Losers to new members in general; nominated with primary	29	28	34	18
Losers to candidate who lost to new member in general	87	65	89	41
New member unopposed in general	0	0	2	0
Open seat; new members had no primary	8	10	15	4
Losers nominated without primary	4	5	7	3
Losers nominated with primary	4	5	9	1
Losers to those nominated in primary above	8	6	15	3
Incumbent winners in Louisiana's "non-partisan" primary facing opposition	6	5	6	5
Losers to these	11	8	10	7

Incumbent winners in Louisiana with no opposition	1	1	2	3
Incumbents losing in a run-off primary in Louisiana with new member from same party	0	1	0	0
Lost in primary	0	4	0	0
Open seat winners in Louisiana	1	1	0	0
Lost runoff to above	1	0	0	0
Losers in primary	7	1	0	0

changes in financing laws had significant impact on how campaigns were run.

Three sets of congressional primaries have been held since that analysis was undertaken. Any review of those elections leads to the conclusion that 1978 was not an atypical year. The primary experiences of candidates in 1978, 1980, 1982, and 1984 are summarized in Table 8.1.

Political scientists have commented for some time that incumbent members of Congress are difficult to unseat. (See the entries in the Supplementary Bibliography as well as those referred to earlier.) These data reveal that the primary process contributes little to incumbent vulnerability.

First, approximately 40 members of the 96th, 97th, and 98th Congresses were re-elected without any competition at all. That is, these incumbents won their party's nomination without opposition and faced no opposition from the other major party in the general election.[2] When the candidates who did face primary opposition but who faced no opposition in the general election are added to this group, approximately 50 members of each Congress have known they would return to the next Congress before the general election was held.

Of the other incumbents seeking re-election, the vast majority did not face opposition for their party's nomination. In each of the three years examined, more than 200 members fall into this category. On the other hand, only in 1984 did more than 100 incumbents who went on to be re-elected face primary opposition. The lesson here seems quite clear. Incumbent members of Congress are difficult to beat. If they are difficult to beat in general elections, they are even more difficult to beat in primaries. Therefore, the smart politician does not try.

Those who seek evidence about the invulnerability of incumbents in primaries cannot find explanatory data as powerful as that which relates to general elections. The conclusions drawn about the advantages of in-

2. As was the case in Chapter 1, this discussion excludes candidates in Louisiana's "nonpartisan" primary.

cumbency from studies of general elections reveal the inability of challengers to offset recognition advantages held by incumbents, and would seem to apply even more so to primary elections, when the elections themselves, not just the candidates, tend to be less visible. Clearly the results of recent primaries would point to the futility of challenging incumbents. In 1980, only six incumbents lost in primaries; small as that number is, it is higher than the total number of incumbent losers in 1982 and 1984 combined.

In almost every case in which an incumbent has lost a primary, obvious local reasons explain that loss. Scandals provide one kind of example, but perhaps the more representative case is that of Congresswoman Katie Hall (D., Ind.). Hall was tapped for the First District nomination in Indiana in 1982, after Congressman Adam Benjamin, Jr. (D., Ind., 1976-1982) died unexpectedly. Hall, the first black to represent Gary in the Congress, was nominated by the local Democratic Party Committee, headed by Gary Mayor Richard Hatcher, because Benjamin's death occurred after the 1982 Indiana primary. Although she won the 1982 general election, her margin was not so great as that normally enjoyed by Benjamin, and she never cemented party support.

In 1984, Hall was challenged by two white, male candidates — Lake County prosecutor Jack Crawford, who was thought to be her most serious challenger, and Peter Visclosky, an attorney and former aide to Benjamin. Hall concentrated her campaign efforts on turning out a large black vote in Gary; Hatcher and his organization and the Reverend Jesse Jackson aided her in this effort. Crawford tried to maintain his early strength based on name recognition, and to prevent whites from deserting him for Visclosky. Visclosky, on the other hand, ran a strong grassroots campaign throughout the district. The vote split almost evenly in three directions, with Visclosky beating Hall by about 2,000 votes and Crawford by 4,000 out of more than 130,000 cast.[3] This case is also interesting because it is one of the few in which an incumbent was beaten despite the fact that she could split her opposition among a number of challengers.

The data also reveal that incumbents' advantages discourage competition for the right to oppose incumbents. In every year more than half of those who faced incumbents in general elections faced no primary competition for their party's nomination. In 1984 the number of nominees running against winning incumbents who did face primary competition rose to nearly as many as those who did not. This might reflect the fact

3. Though a discussion of the run-off primary, hotly debated during the 1984 presidential campaign, is beyond the scope of this analysis, it should be pointed out that, had Hall managed to hold off the challenge of Visclosky and Crawford in the first primary, she almost definitely would have lost in a run-off, if such a situation existed in Indiana. While the situation is hypothetical in this case, it does demonstrate how a minority candidate nearly

Table 8.2 **Primaries in Districts in Which Incumbents Lost General Elections**

a. Incumbents' Nominations

	1978	1980	1982	1984
Incumbent had contested primary	6	11	4	6
Incumbent had no contested primary	13	15	19	10
Total	19	26	23	16

b. Nomination of New Member Who Beat Incumbent

	1978	1980	1982	1984
New member had contested primary	14	15	16	8
New member had no contested primary	5	11	7	8
Total	19	26	23	16

that more Republicans saw incumbent Democrats as vulnerable in the wake of an anticipated Reagan re-election landslide. It is doubtful, however, especially given the continued success of incumbents seeking re-election, that such optimism will constitute the beginning of a trend.

Two additional aspects of the role of primaries in the electoral process deserve attention. First, though few incumbents have lost general elections, it is worthwhile to ask whether primaries played a role in those defeats. Table 8.2 (a) addresses this question. One could hypothesize that incumbents "wounded" in divisive primaries would be most vulnerable in general elections. However, in each case more of the incumbent losers did not have primaries at all than did, though these data do not speak to the divisiveness of the primaries faced by those who did have contests for renomination and who eventually lost.

Table 8.2 (b) looks at the primary routes of the new members who beat incumbents in 1980, 1982, and 1984. One could argue that primaries are beneficial for candidates running against incumbents because the press pays some attention to contested primaries and thus candidate name recognition is increased. Or one could argue that contested primaries are detrimental because they split the opposition to the incumbent. Table 8.2 (b) reveals that both patterns have been followed. It is not very satisfying to conclude that local factors are always important and that generalizations cannot be drawn, but that seems to be the case with this analysis. Before determining whether a contested primary is beneficial or detrimental to a challenger to an incumbent member of Congress, one must have knowledge of a series of related factors about the race at hand — the

led a three-person field (actually a fourth candidate was in the race and drew about 2,000 votes), despite the fact that she could not have achieved a majority.

Table 8.3 **Primaries in Open Seats**

	1978	1980	1982	1984
Winner had contested primary	49	38	49	22
Winner had no contested primary	8	10	15	4
Loser had contested primary	33	33	43	19
Loser had no contested primary	24	15	22	7

timing of the primary, the vulnerability of the incumbent within his/her own party, the media market in the district, the strength of party organization, and many more. Generalizations which ignore these and other factors disregard the real stuff of congressional politics.

Finally, one should look at the role of primaries in open seats, those seats vacated by retiring members of Congress. Nominations in both parties are frequently contested in primary elections in these districts. This is particularly true of the party of the retiring incumbent. This finding is not surprising; it is directly in line with those of others who examine the strategies of congressional candidates (Jacobson, 1983; Jacobson and Kernell, 1981). Candidates are more likely to enter a race when the likelihood of winning is increased. Not only are more of those nominations contested, but they are contested by more candidates. Again, that is the finding which one would expect. Table 8.3 summarizes these data.

CONCLUSIONS

The conclusions which I draw with six years' hindsight are not very different from those which I drew when writing the first edition of this book. The success of our democracy continues to depend on qualified people being willing to serve in challenging offices, and on the electorate having the opportunity to judge among those seeking to represent them.

The primary process is relied upon to narrow the field so that the electorate can choose more thoughtfully. The primary process is only partially successful in fulfilling this function. Many nominations go uncontested. Many of the contests which appear on paper are only perfunctory challenges to overwhelming favorites. The advantages which incumbents have in general elections are magnified in primaries, magnified to the point that only a handful of incumbents lose in every election cycle, and this is so apparent to those in the political arena that few are even challenged.

Moreover, the path to election and the road which one must continue on if one is to remain in office is so difficult to navigate, and the costs of entering on that path and staying on the road are so high, that fewer and fewer are willing to seek election to the Congress or to stay in Congress once elected. How best to recruit and retain those most qualified to govern remains one of the enduring questions facing our nation.

Appendix I

CONGRESSIONAL PRIMARY QUESTIONNAIRE

INSTRUCTIONS: This questionnaire has been designed to gather as much information as possible, while taking as little of your time as possible. Thus, the basic format is multiple choice. However, I want to emphasize that I would very much appreciate any comments you might want to add on any question that you feel needs amplification.

For most questions, the potential answers are preceded by numbers. You should circle the *one* number that corresponds to the most appropriate answer, except in those few cases when the question specifically says that you may circle more than one number. A few questions call for you to enter numbers as the response; in those cases lines have been provided on which to record your answers.

PART I: THE DECISION TO RUN

1. When did you first think that you might run for Congress at some time? Enter the year below.

_____

2. When did you firmly decide that you were going to run in 1978? Enter the month and year below.

_____

3. Was this your first campaign for Congress?
   1. yes
   2. no
   3a. If *NO*, when did you run before? Enter the year(s).

_____

4. Have you run for any other public office?
   1. yes
   2. no
   4a. If *YES*, what office(s) have you sought? Circle all that apply.
      1. local office
      2. state representative
      3. state senator
      4. statewide office
      5. other (please specify)

_____

5. When did you publicly announce your decision to run? Enter the month and year below.

_____

6. When you announced your decision to run, what chance did you think you had to win the primary?
   1. no chance
   2. remote chance
   3. fair chance
   4. good chance
   5. certain of victory
   6. didn't think there would be a primary

7. When you announced your decision to run, how certain were you of whom your opponents would be?
   1. certain of all opponents
   2. certain of major opponents
   3. certain of some major opponents, not others
   4. uncertain of who would run

8. How did you go about assessing your chances in the primary? Circle only major means of assessment.
   1. relied on my political intuition
   2. talked with political leaders and those who know such things
   3. relied on media assessment
   4. conducted a poll
   5. other (please specify below)

Please elaborate on this question if possible:

9. When you announced your decision to run, what chance did you think you had to win the general election if you won the primary?
   1. knew I would lose the primary
   2. no chance in the general election
   3. remote chance in the general election
   4. fair chance in the general election
   5. good chance in the general election
   6. certain of victory in the general election

10. Many people desire to serve in the Congress, but far fewer take the major step of actually running. Assuming your desire to serve, why did you decide to run in 1978?
   1. felt certain I would win
   2. felt it would be my best chance to win
   3. felt an obligation to present an alternative
   4. felt it was something I had to do at some time
   5. felt it would be good for me professionally
   6. felt it would help to build a base for the future
   7. felt a need to air certain views
   8. other (please specify below)

Realizing that this is perhaps the most difficult and personal question I will ask, I again want to emphasize that you should feel free to elaborate more fully.

11. Now that your campaign is over, how do you assess your original decision to run?
    1. right decision for me at time
    2. wrong decision, assessed situation incorrectly
    3. wrong decision, had inadequate information
    4. wrong decision, other reason (please specify below)

    _____

    _____

12. How did your family respond to your decision to run?
    1. enthusiastically encouraging
    2. encouraging, no enthusiasm
    3. indifferent
    4. unenthusiastic, unencouraging, but agreeable
    5. opposed
    6. cannot generalize

Use these same six answers for the next two questions as well.

13. How did your friends respond to your decision to run. Enter number of answer as listed in Question 12.

    _____

14. How did local political leaders respond to your decision to run. Again, please enter number of answer as listed in Question 12.

    _____

15. Did you discuss your decision to run with any of your opponents or perspective opponents before you decided to run?
    1. yes
    2. no
    15a. If *YES,* why, and what was the outcome of those discussions?

    _____

    _____

    _____

    _____

PART II: FINANCING THE CAMPAIGN

1. How much did you expect your campaign to cost? On this and subsequent questions concerning money, please enter dollar figures to the nearest $1,000 unless otherwise specified.

   $ _____ ,000

2. How much did your campaign eventually cost? (I want to reemphasize that all answers will remain confidential.)

   $ _____ ,000

3. How much did you contribute to your campaign (including loans)?

   $ _____ ,000

4. How much did your family contribute?

   $ _____ ,000

5. How much did you raise from other sources?

   $ _____ ,000

6. Approximately what percentage of the total raised came from each of the following? Enter estimate of percentages on the lines provided.

   a. self _____ %

   b. family _____ %

   c. individuals giving $25 or less _____ %

   d. individuals giving $25 to $100 _____ %

   e. individuals giving over $100 but less than $1,000 _____ %

   f. individuals giving $1,000 _____ %

   g. group contributions _____ %

   h. major fundraising events, e.g., concerts _____ %

7. How did you go about raising money? Circle all that apply.
   1. personal appeals to friends
   2. appeals to organized groups
   3. appeals to individuals based on membership in groups
   4. mass mailings
   5. small fundraising events, e.g., cocktail parties
   6. large fundraising events, e.g., concerts
   7. other (please specify below)

   _____

8. How difficult did you find it to raise money?
   1. very difficult
   2. quite difficult
   3. fairly difficult
   4. slightly difficult
   5. no problem

9. What other major races were being run in your district in your party
   at the same time as your primary?
   1. U.S. Senate primary
   2. gubernatorial primary
   3. both of above
   4. other (please specify below)

   _____

   5. no other major primaries

10. Did you or your principle campaign committee have a debt remaining
    at the end of your campaign?
    1. yes
    2. no
    10a. If *YES*, what was the approximate amount of the debt?

       $_____ ,000

    10b. If *YES* to Question 10, how do you intend to pay it off?
       1. personally
       2. more fundraising
       3. other (please specify below)

       _____

11. Did you feel your campaign was adequately financed?
    1. yes

2. no
11a. If *NO*, how much more would you have needed to do the job
you wanted?

$ \underline{\hspace{6cm}} ,000

11b. If you lost, would you have won had you raised that additional
amount?
1. won without it
2. yes, definitely
3. yes, probably
4. unable to say
5. probably not
6. definitely not

12. What role did money play in the outcome of your campaign?
1. no importance
2. little importance
3. considerable importance
4. determining factor

13. Was there a difference in cost between the primary campaigns in your
district in 1978 and those in 1976?
1. yes, more spent in 1978 by far
2. yes, more in 1978 by a little
3. yes, more in 1976 by far
4. yes, more in 1976 by a little
5. no, about the same spent
6. no primaries in 1976
7. don't know

14. Were Federal Election Commission regulations and the restrictions
imposed by law constricting on the way you financed your campaign?
1. yes, definitely
2. yes, slightly
3. no

15. How difficult did you find it to comply with FEC regulations and reporting requirements?
1. not at all difficult
2. slightly difficult
3. fairly difficult
4. extremely difficult

Please elaborate if possible.

PART III: CAMPAIGN ORGANIZATION

1. Did you have the support of the local party organization in your primary?
   1. yes, formal endorsement
   2. yes, but not formally
   3. it was divided
   4. organization stayed neutral
   5. no, an opponent had support
   6. no viable organization exists

2. Who served as your campaign manager?
   1. I did it myself
   2. a relative
   3. a friend
   4. a business associate
   5. a professional manager
   6. other (please specify below)

   _____

   2a. Did this person serve throughout the primary?
       1. yes
       2. no
   2b. If *NO* to Question 2a, please state why not.

3. Approximately how many paid employees worked on your campaign?

   _____

4. What was your total weekly payroll at its peak. Enter the approximate amount to the nearest $100.

   $_____ .00

5. Approximately how many volunteers worked full-time on your campaign for at least one month?

   _____

6. Approximately how many volunteers worked at least twenty hours a week during the last month of your campaign, in addition to those counted above?

   _____

7. Did you hire any political consultants during your primary?
   1. yes
   2. no
   7a. If *YES*, what activities did they help with?

   _____

   7b. If *YES*, how would you evaluate their performance?
       1. excellent
       2. very good
       3. good
       4. fair
       5. poor
       6. used more than one, mixed rating

8. Here is a list of some campaign activities. Please place a check mark
   (✔) to show who had the primary responsibility for each activity
   during your campaign. If primary responsibility was shared, check
   more than one.

	self	paid staff/ consultants	volunteers	not done
a. scheduling				
b. advance work				
c. fundraising				
d. press relations				
e. issue development				
f. issue research				
g. speech writing				
h. advertising design				
i. advertising buying				
j. organizing field				
k. polling				
l. organizing phoning				
m. phoning				
n. FEC compliance				

9. Here is another list of various elements in a campaign. Please place
   a check mark (✔) next to the three or four elements that:
   a. helped your campaign most;
   b. were least helpful in your campaign;

    c.   were done most differently by you from previous campaigns in your district; and

    d.   your opponent(s) did most better than you.

	a. helped	b. least helpful	c. different	d. opponent(s) better
a. use of demographic research and issues				
b. personal performance of candidate				
c. ability to raise funds locally				
d. ability to raise funds elsewhere				
e. use of volunteers				
f. use of campaign brochures, etc.				
g. campaign commercials				
h. compliance with campaign laws				
i. targeting voters				
j. coverage by media				
k. selection and use of paid staff				
l. maintaining financial records				
m. voter registration				
n. NONE				
o. NOT SURE				

10. How long would you say you were actually running for Congress?

_____ months

11. Did you continue on some other job during the primary?
    1.   yes, full-time
    2.   yes, part-time
    3.   no outside job

    11a. *If you continued in another job,* how many hours a week did you campaign during the month before the primary?

_____ hours

11b. During the preceding five months?

_____ hours

11c. *If you did not hold another job,* how long before the primary did you leave your job?

_____

11d. For those who did not hold another job during the primary, how many hours a week did you campaign during the month preceding the election?

_____ hours

11e. During the preceding five months?

_____ hours

12. Below are listed some activities that candidates frequently engage in during a primary campaign. Please check (✓) the appropriate box showing how often you engaged in each activity, if you did it at all.

	nearly every day	many times a week	about once a week	some-times	almost never	never
a. visiting factories and/ or gates						
b. visiting shopping areas						
c. door-to-door						
d. office work on organizations						
e. office work on issues						
f. meeting key people						
g. speeches, etc.						
h. coffees, parties						
i. political party functions						
j. travel						
k. other (please specify below)						
_____						

13. Below are listed some problems that others have had in organizing primary campaigns. Put a check mark (✔) under the appropriate columns.

	serious problem	fairly difficult	slightly difficult	no problem at all
a. securing voting lists				
b. drafting volunteers				
c. raising money				
d. finding a campaign manager				
e. finding a finance manager				
f. having enough personal time				
g. other (please specify below) _____				

PART IV: STRATEGY AND TACTICS

1. Did you commission a public opinion poll before or during your primary?
   1. yes (answer Questions 1a, 1b, 1c)
   2. no (answer Question 1d)

1a. If *YES* to Question 1, was it a professional poll, an amateur poll, or some combination, e.g., a poll written by a professional but administered by volunteer pollsters?
   1. professional
   2. amateur
   3. combination

1b. What was the purpose of the poll? Circle all that apply.
   1. determine if viable candidate
   2. name recognition
   3. issue development
   4. spot opponents' weaknesses
   5. resource allocation
   6. targeting voters
   7. other (please specify below)

1c. If *YES* to Question 1, how important was the poll in your later decisionmaking?
   1. very important
   2. quite important
   3. of some importance
   4. not important at all
1d. If *NO* to Question 1, why did you decide not to conduct a poll?
   1. too expensive
   2. didn't have the time
   3. didn't feel the results would be helpful
   4. don't believe in polling
   5. other (please specify below)

_____

2. How often did you consult with each of the following when deciding strategy?

	daily	weekly	monthly	on occasion	almost never	never
a. campaign manager						
b. other paid staff						
c. volunteers						
d. consultants						
e. public relations firm						
f. pollster						
g. family						
h. business associate						
i. party leaders						
j. others (please specify below)						

3. From the list above, who was your most important adviser in terms of whom you consulted most often?

_____

4. From that same list, who was your most important adviser in terms of who gave you the best advice?

_____

5. What were the major themes of your primary campaign?

_____

_____

6. Were these themes designed for the primary electorate, the general electorate, or was there no difference between the two?
   1. primary electorate
   2. general electorate
   3. no difference

7. Did you campaign aggressively *against* your primary opponents, *for* certain things you stand for, or both?
   1. against primary opponent(s)
   2. for my own positions
   3. both
   7a. *TO BE ANSWERED IF PRIMARY WAS AGAINST AN INCUMBENT*
      Was the incumbent's record an issue in the campaign?
      1. yes
      2. no
   7b. *TO BE ANSWERED IF INCUMBENT WAS RUNNING IN OTHER PARTY*
      Did you or your opponent(s) attack the incumbent during your primary?
      1. yes, everyone did
      2. yes, only I did
      3. yes, only opponent(s) did
      4. no, incumbent not an issue

PART V: MEDIA AND ADVERTISING

1. Did you hire a public relations firm or an advertising firm to help in your primary campaign?
   1. yes (answer Questions 1a-1e)
   2. no (go to Question 2)
   1a. If *YES*, when did you hire the firm?
      1. early in the campaign
      2. in midcampaign
      3. late in the campaign
   1b. What aspects of the campaign were they involved in? Circle all that apply.
      1. strategy setting
      2. producing campaign material

     3.   media presentation
     4.   consulting on some aspects
     5.   other (please specify below)

_____

1c. Was the firm you selected a local firm or a national firm?
     1.   local
     2.   national
1d. Was the firm you selected primarily a political public relations firm or was it one engaged in more general business?
     1.   primarily political
     2.   more general
1e. How would you evaluate the job it did for you?
     1.   excellent
     2.   very good
     3.   good
     4.   only fair
     5.   poor

2. Below are listed a number of items sometimes used in campaigns. On the lines provided, please enter "1" if you used the item or "2" if you did not.

    a.   buttons _____

    b.   bumper stickers _____

    c.   road or house signs _____

    d.   handcards _____

    e.   brochures _____

    f.   other handouts (please specify below)

_____   _____

    g.   Approximately how much money did you spend on the items listed above?

$ _____

3. Did you advertise in newspapers?
     1.   yes (answer Questions 3a-3c)

    2.   no (go to Question 4)

  3a. If *YES*, was this advertising in daily newspapers, weekly newspapers, or both?
       1.   dailies
       2.   weeklies
       3.   both

  3b. Did you use advertising in newspapers throughout your campaign or mostly at the end?
       1.   throughout the campaign
       2.   primarily at the end

  3c. Approximately how much money did you spend on newspaper advertising?

$ _____

4.   Did you advertise on radio during your primary?
     1.   yes (answer Questions 4a-4c)
     2.   no (go to Question 5)

  4a. If *YES*, how many separately designed spots did you use? Enter the number of each.
       1.   10-second spots   _____

       2.   30-second spots   _____

       3.   1- minute spots   _____

       4.   longer spots   _____

  4b. On how many radio stations did you advertise?

_____ stations

  4c. Approximately how much money did you spend on radio advertising?

$ _____

5.   Did you advertise on television during your primary campaign?
     1.   yes (answer Questions 5a-5c)
     2.   no (go to Question 6)

  5a. If *YES*, how many separately designed spots did you use? Enter the number of each.
       1.   l0-second spots   _____

       2.   30- second spots   _____

3. 1-minute spots   _____

4. longer spots   _____

5b. On how many television stations did you advertise?

_____ stations

5c. Approximately how much money did you spend on television advertising?

$ _____

6. Did you use direct mail advertising during your primary campaign?
    1. yes (answer Questions 6a-6c)
    2. no (go to Question 7)

    6a. If *YES*, were the mailings district-wide or to selected lists?
         1. district-wide
         2. selected lists
         3. some of each.

    6b. How many such mailings did you sent out?

    _____ mailings

    6c. Approximately how much money did you spend on direct mail?

    $ _____

7. Did you use billboard or public transit advertising during your primary campaign?
    1. yes
    2. no

    7a. If *YES*, approximately how much money did you spend on these?

    $ _____

8. Please list any other major advertising expenses that you incurred and the amount spent on these.

9. Approximately how many press conferences did you hold during the campaign?

_____ press conferences

PLEASE GO TO QUESTION 9A IF YOU HELD PRESS CONFER-
ENCES: GO TO QUESTION 10 IF YOU DID NOT HOLD PRESS
CONFERENCES.

9a. If you held press conferences, how would you evaluate the
coverage they received by the various media? Enter the appropriate number on the lines provided.
1. always well attended
2. sometimes well attended, sometimes not
3. never well attended
a. by print media   _____

b. by radio stations   _____

c. by television stations   _____

9b. How effective were these press conferences in attracting attention to your campaign?
1. very effective
2. somewhat effective
3. not very effective
4. very ineffective
9c. If they were not very effective, can you state why?

10. How often did you issue press releases during your campaign?
1. daily
2. a couple a week
3. about once a week
4. a couple a month
5. less frequently than that
6. never
10a. How often were these releases successful in gaining you publicity? Use the numbers below to evaluate effectiveness for the
various media at various stages in the campaign.
1. always
2. frequently
3. sometimes
4. infrequently
5. never

	wire services	dailies	weeklies	radio	TV
a. early in the campaign b. last month of campaign c. last week of campaign					

12. How frequently did you debate your opponent(s) during the campaign?
    Enter the number of debates or joint appearances.

    _____ debates

    12a. How many of these were televised?

    _____

    12b. How many were on radio?

    _____

    12c. How many were covered in the daily newspapers?

    _____

13. Generally, how would you evaluate the coverage given your primary by the local media?
    1. excellent
    2. very good
    3. good
    4. only fair
    5. poor

PART VI: AFTER THE CAMPAIGN

1. Did you endorse the eventual winner publicly?
    1. I was the winner (go to Question 4)
    2. yes (answer Questions 2 and 3)
    3. no (answer Questions 2 and 3)

2. Did you work actively in his or her campaign?
    1. yes
    2. no

3. Did your supporters work for the eventual winner?
   1. yes, with enthusiasm
   2. yes, but unenthusiastically
   3. only for appearances' sake
   4. some did, others not at all
   5. few if any worked in the general

THOSE ANSWERING QUESTIONS 2 AND 3, G0 T0 QUESTION 6.

4. *FOR PRIMARY WINNERS ONLY*
   Did your opponent(s) work actively and publicly for your election?
   1. yes
   2. some did, others not
   3. no

5. *FOR PRIMARY WINNERS ONLY*
   Did your opponents' supporters work in your general election effort?
   1. yes, with enthusiasm
   2. yes, but unenthusiastically
   3. only for appearances' sake
   4. some did, others not
   5. few if any

6. *ALL ANSWER THIS AND FOLLOWING*
   Would you say that your primary was a divisive one or not?
   1. divisive
   2. not divisive

7. What effect did you feel the primary contest had on your party's chances in the general?
   1. enhanced chances of winning
   2. had little or no effect
   3. hurt party's chances

8. How satisfied were you with the primary campaign you ran?
   1. totally satisfied
   2. generally satisfied
   3. partially satisfied
   4. not at all satisfied

9. After this experience, what is your general feeling about running for public office?
   1. very beneficial personal experience

2. many good aspects, but high personal costs
3. personal costs too high

10. Do you think you will ever run for Congress again?
    1. yes, in 1980
    2. yes, sometime
    3. probably sometime
    4. unlikely
    5. definitely not

11. Do you think you will ever seek another elective office?
    1. yes, definitely
    2. probably
    3. unlikely
    4. definitely not

12. What effect did your campaign have on your personal career development?
    1. enhanced it
    2. no effect
    3. detrimental effect

THANK YOU VERY MUCH FOR TAKING THE TIME AND EFFORT TO COMPLETE THIS QUESTIONNAIRE. PLEASE RETURN IT IN THE ENCLOSED, STAMPED ENVELOPE TO:

SANDY MAISEL
DEPARTMENT OF GOVERNMENT
COLBY COLLEGE
WATERVILLE, MAINE 04901

AGAIN, MY SINCEREST THANKS FOR YOUR COOPERATION.

Appendix II

COMMERCIALS USED IN MAISEL FOR CONGRESS CAMPAIGN

SAMPLE THIRTY-SECOND TELEVISION SPOT

Video	*Audio*
	NARRATOR:
Maisel talking to factory worker.	A worker for more jobs, Sandy Maisel.
Maisel eating with elderly group.	A voice for national health insurance, Sandy Maisel.
Maisel teaching in classroom.	A teacher for tomorrow's leaders, Sandy Maisel.
Maisel seated on desk in office.	A Congressman for Maine, Sandy Maisel.
	SANDY MAISEL:
	I'm Sandy Maisel. I not only teach government, I work very hard to reform it. We all care about the future of Maine. During the course of this campaign, I'll discuss ways to improve the quality of life for all of us.
Graphic	NARRATOR:
When you know Sandy Maisel, you'll want him in Congress.	When you know Sandy Maisel, you'll want him in Congress.

Paid for by the Maisel for Congress
Committee.

SAMPLE THIRTY-SECOND RADIO SPOTS
"Bread & Butter"

MAISEL:
I'm Sandy Maisel, Democrat for Congress. I'm concerned about a bread-and-butter issue.

Bread and butter.

It takes jobs to put them on our tables. David Emery's vote on the jobs bill cost Maine two million dollars.

He voted wrong again by supporting a give-away for cotton and wheat growers that would have hurt Maine's farmers and Maine's consumers.

We need a congressman who cuts waste, not just ribbons at supermarket openings.

I'll work hard to cut the costs that hurt you!

ANNOUNCER:
Now that you know Sandy Maisel, you can put him in Congress.

Paid for by the Maisel for Congress Committee.

"Maine's Economy"

MAISEL:
I'm Sandy Maisel, Democrat for Congress. I want to get Maine's economy moving again.

We need our fair share of federal dollars and constructive new ideas. We're not getting either one from our congressman now!

We need economic development funds to strengthen industries already here . . . seed money to diversify and revitalize our fishing industry.

And we need new industry, too. Improving our railbeds and lowering shipping costs would help.

With your vote I'll work to get Maine's economy moving again!

ANNOUNCER:
Now that you know Sandy Maisel, you can put him in Congress.

Paid for by the Maisel for Congress Committee.

"Experience"

MAISEL:
I'm Sandy Maisel, Democrat for Congress.

I know how to get results in Washington. Recently, congressional leaders asked me to work with them to make the House more efficient and more accountable to taxpayers.

David Emery voted against even debating whether members of Congress should tell us how much of our money their trips cost.

I can work effectively to end waste in government — (pause) — to end abuse by government officials, especially members of Congress. That's why I want your vote.

ANNOUNCER:
Now that you know Sandy Maisel, you can put him in Congress.
Paid for by the Maisel for Congress Committee.

"Jobs"

MAISEL:
From Belfast to Biddeford, Pittston to Portland, Wiscasset to Waterville, there's a deep and growing concern about jobs and the ever-rising cost of living.

I know. I've heard it firsthand from First District voters. I'm Sandy Maisel, Democrat for Congress. That's why I'm pledged to get Maine's economy moving again.

I'll make it my first order of business to make sure Maine's families can meet today's needs with decent incomes from secure jobs and can plan for a better future, too.

ANNOUNCER:
Now that you know Sandy Maisel, you can put him in Congress.
Paid for by the Maisel for Congress Committee.

"Health Care"

MAISEL:
I'm Sandy Maisel, Democrat for Congress, and I'm concerned with the cost and quality of health care for Maine.

That's why I have suggested health insurance programs that would assist those whose health care needs are not in keeping with their ability to pay:

Our senior citizens who are beyond their peak earning years and now struggle to exist on low, fixed incomes.

Our children, under age eight, because it has been proved that they are the most effective target for preventive-medicine programs.

ANNOUNCER:
Now that you know Sandy Maisel, you can put him in Congress.
Paid for by the Maisel for Congress Committee.

SELECTED BIBLIOGRAPHY

The professional literature on congressional primaries is very slim. The works listed below are those that have been referred to in the text and others that have been used to structure my research and thinking on this topic and that I feel will be useful to others pursuing this field.

Abramowitz, A.I. (1981) "Party and individual accountability in the 1978 congressional elections," in L.S. Maisel and J. Cooper, eds., *Congressional Elections*. Beverly Hills: Sage.

———— (1975) "Name familiarity, reputation, and the incumbency effect in a congressional election." *Western Pol. Q.* 28 (Dec.): 668-84.

Ackerman, D. (1957) "Significance of congressional races with identical candidates in successive district elections." *Midwest J. of Pol. Sci.* I (Aug.): 173-80.

Agranoff, R. (1976) *The Management of Election Campaigns*. Boston: Holbrook.

Arsenau R., and R. Wolfinger (1973) "Voting behavior in congressional elections," presented at the annual meeting of the American Political Science Association, New Orleans.

Asher, H.B., and H.F. Weisberg (1978) "Voting change in Congress: Some dynamic perspectives on an evolutionary process." *Amer. J. of Pol. Sci.* 22 (May): 391-425.

Bass, J., and W. de Vries (1976) *The Transformation of Southern Politics*. New York: Basic Books.

Bernstein, R.A. (1977) "Divisive primaries do hurt: U.S. Senate races, 1956-1972." *Amer. Pol. Sci. Rev.* 71 (June): 540.

Bicker, W.E. (1972) "Ideology is alive and well in California: Party identification, issue positions, and voting behavior," presented at the annual meeting of the American Political Science Association, Washington, D.C.

Born, R. (1980) "Changes in the competitiveness of House primary elections, 1956-1976." *Amer. Pol. Q.* 8 (Oct.): 495-506.

———— (1979) "Generational replacement and the growth of incumbent reelection margins in the U.S. House." *Amer. Pol. Sci. Rev.* 73 (Sept.): 811-17.

———— (1977) "House incumbents and inter-election vote change." *J. of Politics* 39 (Nov.): 1008-34.

Burnham, W.D. (1975) "Insulation and responsiveness in Congressional elections." *Pol. Sci. Q.* 90 (Fall): 411-35.

Campbell, A., P.E. Converse, W.E. Miller, and D.E. Stokes (1960) *The American Voter.* New York: Wiley.

Clapp, C. (1963) *The Congressman: His Work as He Sees It.* Washington, D.C.: Brookings.

Clem, A.L., ed. (1976) *The Making of Congressmen: Seven Campaigns of 1974.* North Scituate, Mass.: Duxbury.

Converse, P.E., and G.B. Markus (1979) "Plus a ca change . . .: The new CPS election study panel." *Amer. Pol. Sci. Rev.* 73 (March): 32-49.

Cook, R. (1978) "Why some House members lose in primaries." *Cong. Q.* 36:42 (Oct. 21): 3062.

Cooper, J., and W. West (1981) "The congressional career in the 1970s," in L.C. Dodd and B.I. Oppenheimer, eds., *Congress Reconsidered,* 2d ed. Washington, D.C.: Congressional Quarterly Press.

Cover, A.D. (1977) "One good term deserves another: The advantage of incumbency in congressional elections." *Amer. J. of Pol. Sci.* 21 (Aug.): 523-42.

Cover, A.D., and D.R. Mayhew (1977) "Congressional dynamics and the decline of competitive congressional elections," in L.C. Dodd and B.I. Oppenheimer, eds., *Congress Reconsidered.* New York: Praeger.

Cox, E. (1962) "Congressional district party strengths and the 1960 election." *J. of Pol.* 24 (May): 277-302.

Crotty, W.J. (1980) *The Party Symbol.* San Francisco: W.H. Freeman.

Crotty, W.J., and G.C. Jacobson (1980) *American Parties in Decline.* Boston: Little, Brown.

Cummings, M.C. (1966) *Congressmen and the Electorate.* New York: Free Press.

Donovan, J. (1958) *Congressional Campaign: Maine Elects a Democrat.* New York: Holt, Rinehart.

Erikson, R.S. (1971) "The advantage of incumbency in congressional elections." *Polity* 3 (Spring): 395-405.

Fenno, R.F., Jr. (1978) *Homestyle: House Members in Their Districts.* Boston: Little, Brown.

———— (1975) "If, as Ralph Nader says, Congress is 'the broken branch,' how come we love our Congressman so much?" in N. Ornstein, ed., *Congress in Change.* New York: Praeger.

Ferejohn, J. (1977) "On the decline of competition in congressional districts."*Amer. Pol. Sci. Ref.* 71 (March): 166-76.

Fiellin, A. (1967) "Recruitment and legislative role conceptions." *Western Pol. Q.* 20 (June): 271-87.

Fiorina, M.P. (1977) *Congress: Keystone of the Washington Establishment.* New Haven: Yale Univ. Press.

Fishel, J. (1973) *Party and Opposition: Congressional Challengers in American Politics.* New York: David McKay.

Fowler, L.L. (1980) "Candidate perceptions of electoral coalitions." *Amer. Pol. Q.* 8 (Oct.): 483-94.

Froman, L.A. (1966) "A realistic approach to campaign strategies and tactics," in M.K. Jennings and J.H. Zeigler, eds., *The Electoral Process.* Englewood Cliffs, N.J.: Prentice-Hall.

Hacker, A. (1965) "Does a 'divisive' primary harm a candidate's election chances?" *Amer. Pol. Sci. Rev.* 59 (March): 105.

Hadley, A. (1976) *The Invisible Primary.* Englewood Cliffs, N.J.: Prentice-Hall

Havard, W.C., ed. (1972) *The Changing Politics of the South.* Baton Rouge: Louisiana State Univ. Press.

Hinckley, B. (1981) "House reelections and Senate defeats: The role of the challenger," in L.S. Maisel and J. Cooper, eds., *Congressional Elections.* Beverly Hills: Sage.

Huckshorn, R.J., and R.C. Spencer (1971) *The politics of Defeat: Campaigning for Congress.* Amherst: Univ. of Massachusetts Press.

Jacobson, G.C. (1981) "Congressional elections, 1978: The case of the vanishing challengers," in L.S. Maisel and J. Cooper, eds., Congressional Elections. Beverly Hills: Sage.

_____ (1980) *Money in Congressional Elections,* New Haven: Yale Univ. Press.

_____ (1978) "The effects of campaign spending in congressional elections." Amer. Pol. Sci. Rev. 72 (June): 469-91.

Jennings, M.K. and L.H. Zeigler, eds. (1966a) *The Electoral Process.* Englewood Cliffs, N.J.: Prentice-Hall.

_____ (1966b) "Class, party and race in four types of elections: The case of Atlanta." *J. of Pol.* 28 (May): 391-407.

_____ (1966c) "Class, party and race in four types of elections: The case of Atlanta." *J. of Pol.* 28 (May): 391-407.

Jewell, M.E., and D.M. Olson (1978) *American State Political Parties and Elections.* Homewood, Ill.: Dorsey.

Johnson, D., and J. Gibson (1974) "The divisive primary revisited: Party activists in Iowa." *Amer. Pol. Sci. Rev.* 68 (March): 67.

Jones, C.O. (1967) *Every Second Year.* Washington, D.C.: Brookings.

_____ (1966) "The role of the campaign in Congressional politics," in M.K. Jennings and L.H. Zeigler, eds., *The Electoral Process.* Englewood Cliffs, N.J.: Prentice-Hall.

_____ (1962) "A suggested scheme for classifying congressional elections." *Pub. Op. Q.* 26 (Spring): 126-32.

Kayden, X. (1978) *Campaign Organization.* Lexington, Mass.: D.C. Heath.

Kazee, T.A. (1980) "The decision to run for the U.S. Congress: Challengers' attitudes in the 1970s." *Legislative Studies Q.* 5 (Feb.): 79-100.

Key, V.O. (1964) *Politics, Parties and Pressure Groups.* New York: Crowell.
_____ (1956) *Southern Politics.* New York: Knopf.
Kingdon, J.W. (1966) *Candidates for Office: Beliefs and strategies.* New York: Random House.
LaFollette, R.M. (1913) *LaFollette's Autobiography.* Madison: R.M. LaFollette.
Leuthold, D. (1968) *Electioneering in a Democracy.* New York: Wiley.
Maisel, L.S. (1981) "Congressional primary elections in 1978." *Amer. Pol. Q.* 9 (Jan.): 23-47.
Maisel, L.S., and J. Cooper (1981) *Congressional Elections.* Beverly Hills: Sage.
Mann, T.E. (1978) *Unsafe at Any Margin: Interpreting Congressional Elections.* Washington, D.C.: American Enterprise Institute.
Mann, T.E., and R.E. Wolfinger (1981) "Candidates and parties in congressional elections," in L.S. Maisel and J. Cooper, eds., *Congressional Elections.* Beverly Hills: Sage.
Mayhew, D.R. (1974a) Congress: *The Electoral Connection.* New Haven: Yale Univ. Press.
_____ (1974b) "Congressional elections: The case of the vanishing marginals." *Polity* 6 (Spring): 295-319.
Moos, M. (1952) Politics, Presidents and Coattails. Baltimore: John Hopkins Univ. Press.
Nelson, C.J. (1978) "The effects of incumbency on voting in congressional elections, 1964-1974." *Pol. Sci. Q.* 93 (Winter): 665-78.
Olson, D.M. (1978) "U.S. Congressmen and their diverse congressional districts." *Legislative Studies Q.* 3 (May): 239-64.
Paletz. D.L. (1971) "The neglected context of congressional campaigns. *Polity* 4 (Winter): 195-217.
Parker, G.R. (1980) "The advantage of incumbency in House elections." *Amer. Pol. Q.* 8 (Oct.): 449-64.
_____ (1981) "Incumbent popularity and electoral success," in L.S. Maisel and J. Cooper, eds., *Congressional Elections.* Beverly Hills: Sage.
Payne, J.L. (1980) "The personal electoral advantage of House incumbents, 1936-1976." *Amer. Pol Q.* 8 (Oct.): 465-82.
Price, H.D. (1965) "The electoral arena," in D.B. Truman, ed., *The Congress and America's Future.* Englewood Cliffs, N.J.: Prentice-Hall.
Ranney, A., and L.D. Epstein (1966) "The two electorates: Voters and non-voters in a Wisconsin primary." *J. of Pol.* 28 (Aug.): 598-616.
Riggs, R. (1963) "The district five primary." *Arizona Rev. of Bus. and Pub. Adm.* (March): 1-14.
Rohde, D.W. (1979) "Risk-bearing and progressive ambition:. The Case of the U.S. House of Representatives." *Amer. J. of Pol. Sci.* 23 (Feb.): 1-26.
Schantz, H.L. (1980) "Contested and uncontested primaries for the U.S. House." *Legislative Studies Q.* 5 (Nov.): 545-62.
_____ (1976) "Julius Turner revisited: Primary elections as an alternative to party competition in 'safe' districts." *Amer. Pol. Sci. Rev.* 70 (June): 541-45.
Shadegg, S.C. (1972) *The New How to Win an Election.* New York: Taplinger.
Snowiss, L.M. (1966) "Congressional recruitment and representation. *Amer. pol. Sci. REv.* 60 (March): 627-39.

Stone, W.J. (1980) "The dynamics of constituency: Electoral control in the House." *Amer. Pol. Q.* 8 (October); 399-424.

Tedin, K., and R. Murray (1979) "Public awareness of congressional representatives: Recall versus recognition' " *Amer. Pol. Q.* 7 (Oct.): 509-17.

Tufte, E.R. (1975) "Determinants of the outcomes of midterm congressional elections." *Amer. Pol. Sci. Rev.* 69 (Sept.): 812-26.

_____ (1973) "The relationship between seats and votes in two-party systems." *Amer. Pol. Sci. Rev.* 68 (June): 540-54.

Witcover, J. (1977) *Marathon: The pursuit of the Presidency, 1972-1976.* New York: Viking.

Wright, G. (1978) "Candidates' policy positions and voting in U.S. congressional elections." *Legislative Studies Q.* 3 (Aug.): 445-64.

SUPPLEMENTARY SELECTED BIBLIOGRAPHY

While primary elections have not been at the forefront of political scientists' research agenda in the last three years, the work on congressional elections continues at a fast pace. Many of the works listed below are valuable for those who are interested in all aspects of the electoral process.

Abramson, P.R., J.H. Aldrich, and D.W. Rohde (1983) *Change and Continuity in the 1980 Election.* Washington, D.C.: Congressional Quarterly Press.

Alexander, H.E. (1984) *Financing Politics: Money, Elections, and Political Reform.* 3d ed. Washington, D.C.: Congressional Quarterly Press.

Clarke, P., and S.H. Evans (1983) *Covering Campaigns: Journalism in Congressional Elections.* Stanford: Stanford Univ. Press.

Copeland, G.W. (1982) "The effects of campaign expenditures on turnout for congressional elections," presented at the annual meeting of the Midwest Political Science Association, Milwaukee.

Cover, A.D., and B.S. Brumberg (1982) "Baby books and ballots: The impact of congressional mail on constituent opinion." *Amer. Pol. Sci. Rev.* (June): 347-59.

Cover, A.D., and D. Mayhew (1981) "Congressional dynamics and the decline of competitive congressional elections," in L.C. Dodd and B.I. Oppenheimer, eds., *Congress Reconsidered,* 2d ed. Washington, D.C.: Congressional Quarterly Press.

Dodd, L.C., and B.I. Oppenheimer (1981) "The House in transition: Change and consolidation." *Congress Reconsidered,* 2d ed. Washington, D.C.: Congressional Quarterly Press.

Fleischman, J.L., ed. (1982) *The Future of American Political Parties: The Quality of Governance.* Englewood Cliffs, N.J.: Prentice-Hall.

Gibson, J.L., C.P. Cotter, J.F. Bibby, and R.J. Huckshorn (1983) "Assessing party organization strength." *Amer J. of Pol. Sci.* 27 (May): 193-222.

_____ (1982) "Whither the local parties? A cross-sectional and longitudinal analysis of the strength of party organizations," presented at the annual meeting of Western Political Science Association, San Diego, Calif.

Goldenberg, E.N., and M.W. Traugott (1984) *Campaigning for Congress.* Washington, D.C.: Congressional Quarterly Press.

_____ (1982) "Campaign managers' perceptions and strategic decisions in congressional elections," presented at the annual meeting of Western Political Science Association, San Diego, Calif.

_____ (1981) "Normal vote analysis of U.S. congressional elections." *Legislative Studies Q.* (May): 247-58.

Goldenberg, E.N., M.W. Traugott, and F.R. Baumgartner (1983) "Preemptive and reactive spending in U.S. House races," presented at the annual meeting of the Midwest Political Science Association, Chicago.

Gopoian, D.J. (1984) "What makes PAC tide?" *Amer. J. of Pol. Sci.* 28 (May): 259-81.

Hershey, M.R. (1984) *Running for Office.* Chatham, N.J.: Chatham House.

Hibbing, J.R. (1982) "Voluntary retirement from the U.S. House of Representatives: Who quits?" *Amer. J. of Pol. Sci.* (Aug.): 467-84.

Hinckley, B. (1981) *Congressional Elections.* Washington, D.C.: Congressional Quarterly Press.

Jacobson, G.C. (1983) *The Politics of Congressional Elections.* Boston: Little, Brown.

Jacobson, G.C., and S. Kernell (1981) *Strategy and Choice in Congressional Elections.* New Haven: Yale Univ. Press.

Johannes, J.R. (1983) "Explaining congressional casework styles." *Amer. J. of Pol. Sci.* 27 (Aug.): 530-47.

Johannes, J.R., and J.C. McAdams (1981) "The congressional incumbency effect: Is it casework, policy compatibility, or something else?" *Amer. J. of Pol. Sci.* (Aug.) 512-42.

Jones, R., and W. Miller (1983) "Financing campaigns: The individual contributor," presented at the annual meeting of the Midwest Political Science Association, Chicago.

Kazee, T.A., and M.C. Thornberry (1983) "Can we throw the rascals out?: Recruiting challengers in competitive districts," presented at the annual meeting of American Political Science Association, Chicago.

Krehbiel, K., and J.R. Wright (1983) "The incumbency effect in congressional elections." *Amer. J. of Pol. Sci.* 27 (Feb.): 140-57.

McAdams, J.C., and J.R. Johannes (1981) "Does casework matter? A reply to Professor Fiorina." *Amer. J. of Pol. Sci.* 25 (Aug.): 581-601.

Malbin, M.J., ed. (1984) *Money in Politics in the United States: Financing Elections in the 1980's.* Chatham, N.J.: Chatham House.

Mandel, R.B. (1981) *In the Running: The New Woman Candidate.* Boston: Beacon Press.

Mann, T.G., and N.J. Ornstein, eds., (1983) *The American Election of 1982.* Washington, D.C.: American Enterprise Institute.

Parker, G.R. (1981) "Interpreting candidate awareness in U.S. congressional elections." *Legislative Studies Q.* (May): 219-33.

Price, D.E. (1984) *Bringing Back the Parties.* Washington, D.C.: Congressional Quarterly Press.

Ragsdale, L. (1981) "Incumbent popularity, challenger, invisibility, and congressional voters." *Legislative Studies Q.* (May): 201-18.

Sabato, L.J. (1984) *PAC Power: Inside the World of Political Action Committees.* New York: Norton.

_____ (1981) *The Rise of Political Consultants.* New York: Basic Books.

Uslaner, E. (1981) "Ain't misbehavin': The logic of defensive issue voting strategies in Congressional elections." *Amer. Pol. Q.* 9 (Jan.): 3-25.

Yiannakis, D.E. (1981) "The grateful electorate: Casework and congressional elections." *Amer. J. of Pol. Sci.* 25 (Aug.): 568-580.

INDEX

From Obscurity to Oblivion has been composed on a Mergenthaler phototypesetter in ten-point Times Roman. Machine Bold type was used as display. The jacket design by Greta Eichel provided the base for the book design by Jim Billingsley. The book was printed offset by Thomson-Shore, Inc., Dexter, Michigan, and bound by John H. Dekker & Sons, Inc., Grand Rapids, Michigan. The paper on which the book is printed bears the watermark of S.D. Warren and is designed for an effective life of at least three hundred years.

THE UNIVERSITY OF TENNESSEE PRESS : KNOXVILLE